MISS
UNIVERSE

is interviewed
on a rooftop.
In the distance to the
left, the Barcelona
Men's Penitentiary
Centre is visible,
popularly known as
La Model prison.

MISS UNIVERSE
Eroticism is an object, a monstrous object.

JOURNALIST
An object?

M.U. Yes, an object. Eroticism is an object of poetic contemplation.

J. Why is it a monstrous object?

M.U. Because it violates us. Eroticism unbalances us and pushes us to consciously question ourselves. It's our problematic self. We tend to deceive ourselves because we believe that what violates us is distant. But no. Eroticism responds to the interior nature of desire. It responds to our intimacy. Eroticism is as violent as desire. We are what we want and that is very violent because not only does it unbalance and push us, it also defines us. It can be avoided, but for people who aren't able to avoid it, eroticism is the intimate and universal problem par excellence.

J. Could you define yourself?

M.U. I'm an erotic object.

J. What is violence in your opinion?

M.U. The mastery of eroticism, its territory, and power.

J. Why?

M.U. Because eroticism arises from the tension between

I

In defense of the artist's abilities and avant-garde, political, and artistic potential and against the artist's current role of capitalist propaganda that simplifies, reduces, and diminishes the artist, condemning the artist, definitively, to commercial mediocrity whether because the State, the elites, or the oligarchies thus decide or because, whether it has been decided so or not, under capitalism, the artist tends to present and represent the bourgeois worldview as unique and absolute, thus contributing to its production and reproduction, and, therefore, to its legitimization, I believe, although humbly and modestly, that without exposing a complete analysis that would entail a meticulous and detailed work that does not interest me at this moment, it is worthwhile and just not to continue contributing, myself, to the classifications and segmentations of cinema that are useless, disadvantageous, and absurd to art and useful, advantageous, and convenient for the market.

Insisting on the categorization of cinematographic expression – which could guide us in reference to gender and format, or style, in another context and from other perspectives that did not endow an artwork with a commodity, that did not allocate it to its commercialization, that did not limit it artistically, consequently – is now if not a symptom of our time, a strategy that aims to maximize the economic value of artistic creation by promoting the diversification of its professionalization and its specialization in the art market and the film industry. Consumption trends and the logic of supply and demand, mutually conditioning, changing, fickle, and volatile, made possible and maintained by the competitiveness and rivalry typical of the capitalist system, demand that art, as a fetish and as a product, adapt to the emergence of different market niches and their respective audiences/consumers in order to ensure its revenue and profit to the detriment of its transcendent potential and its authentic artistic qualities and value.

Since the 60s and 70s, from the beginning of what some call postmodernity – or late capitalism, according to Fredric Jameson, or capitalist realism, according to Mark Fisher – the imperatives of research and experimentation that define all artistic practice, coinciding with the development of technology that has facilitated access to audiovisual media and that have enabled other film distribution and screening procedures, have driven filmmakers to explore new forms, techniques, and visions with respect to those of conventional and commercial cinema. However, all of them have always been subsumed by capitalism, commodified and commercialized, banalized, and standardized. Likely, faced with the question "What is *MISS UNIVERSE*?", a role that I have both directed and played, following a script that I would write myself, would answer: "solely and simply, nothing more and nothing less than a cinematographic work."

II

MISS UNIVERSE is a short film that oscillates between video art and video essay, an independent and experimental film in which authorship, through form and content, declares itself to be feminine, even as it violates and disobeys the clichés and expectations attributed to the superlative, ideal, and exemplary figure that Miss Universe symbolizes for women. Intended to represent their nation and to vulgarly promote a certain empowerment and a certain social conscience serving the economic and political interests of the businessmen who run beauty contests, docile and educated, harmless and grateful, smiling, silly, and superficial, the personification of the greatest female stereotyping today, I thought it was ideal for subverting it and challenging the hypocrisy and moralism that characterize feminism when, without elaborating a critique of capitalist dynamics in relation to gender, it disapproves, reprimands, and blames normatively feminine manifestations.

Feminist art or art created by women has not only become another specialized and specific market, identitarian, which, in this case, is marketed with gender oppression and violence originated by the same system that capitalizes on them, is also instrumentalizing, mystifying, and essentializing a type of supposedly feminine art that, on the one hand, presupposes, marks, and points out, or establishes, what type of art women make or should make and what type of art they consume or desire – or even what they should consume and what they should desire – and, on the other hand, how or what a woman should be through the complete analogy between her consumption and her desire. From a historical and artistic perspective that understands gender statements, in general, and the feminine, in particular, as a sociocultural legacy worthy of being studied, first, and being questioned, subsequently, like any other, and assuming one's own feminine experience – that is, one's own socialization as a heterosexual and normative woman – I decided to film a Miss Universe who, surprisingly, against all macho or feminist pretenses and the market, responded in an interview with the artifice of poetry and the lucidity of philosophy.

Presenting a Miss Universe as a class-conscious proletarian, at the very least, or as a communist militant, at the most, would entail a distancing between her form and her content that, although I would continue to achieve the fantasy and imagination that in my work, consenting to the licenses of fiction, I attempt and pursue, would have meant an association of ideas, easy and vulgar, predictable and literal, far from being able to create a dialectic, because the type of conflicts and contradictions between these two contrary ideas would hinder a deep and effective discussion, would result in a caricature, not in a synthesis, without complexity and without relevance, which would hypocritically annul the raison d'être of the one and the other. Therefore, I invented a historically determined but revolutionarily imagined character: feminine and violent,

what is forbidden and transgression at work, that invention, that consensus that represses and imposes rules of coexistence and takes us away from our violence.

J. From our violence?

M.U. Yes, work structures our lives and distances us from sex and aggression.

J. Are you violent?

M.U. Yes, I'm an erotic object.

J. Do you like your work?

M.U. I don't work. I'm Miss Universe, not working class.

J. What's your opinion on trade unionism?

M.U. I don't like to share my opinions.

J. Are you transgressive?

M.U. Workers aren't in a position to create laws in relation to their labour rights. However, most of them follow them faithfully. I'm not in a position to create laws either, but I never follow them faithfully.

J. Do you consider yourself to be freer than a worker?

M.U. It's not about freedom. There's no prohibition that cannot be transgressed.

J. Do you think transgression and freedom are related?

M.U. Transgression removes prohibition without suppressing it and it's often something, a thing that is admitted, even prescribed.

J. When?

M.U. For example, when the bloodiest of murderers is unable to ignore damnation because damnation is the condition of his glory. But... yes, I am freer than a worker. I don't work. I'm Miss Universe, an erotic object.

J. What laws would you ban?

M.U. Laws are what prohibit.

J. What laws do you hate?

M.U. "*Thou shalt not kill*" and "*Thou shalt not commit adultery*."

J. Would you like to murder someone?

M.U. Yes.

J. Who?

M.U. Desire itself. I live under the totalitarianism of desire.

J. What does desire mean to you?

M.U. Desire isn't understood, it's suffering.

J. Did you work before being chosen Miss Universe?

M.U. Yes, I was a bartender.

J. And what did you do in your free time?

a Miss Universe aware of her own social function, without claiming it and without questioning it, transfiguring it, yes, artistically, intellectually, and sensually, metaphorically, not (only) as an object of consumption, not (only) as a sexual object, not (only) as an object of desire, but as an erotic object.

According to Georges Bataille, eroticism is the object of a poetic contemplation. Only thus interpreted can it be described as the French writer and anthropologist did, beyond sexuality, beyond sexual or physical pleasure, beyond the consummation of desire, broadly speaking, as a radically human phenomenon that explores the limits of existence, such as attraction to the forbidden, such as fusion with the other, such as the dissolution of the self, such as the tension between life and death, connecting the being with its most primitive nature and its most essential drives, impelling it to transgress preestablished laws, norms, and prohibitions in order to preserve the social order. The subversive and, therefore, violent component that Bataille attributes to the erotic is contained and unfolds throughout the entire audiovisual piece, contrasting with the discipline and domestication that, a priori, femininity supposes, in this case, *eroticized*, provocatively challenging when, on unionism, for example, Miss Universe replies: "Workers aren't in a position to create laws in relation to their labour rights. However, most of them follow them faithfully. I'm not in a position to create laws either, but I never follow them faithfully."

Without ignoring the base materialism or the deviant materialism that are at the core of Bataille's studies, addressing the erotic as an object to contemplate and to poeticize reveals the extraordinarily literary and not exclusively philosophical dimension that Bataille proposes when analyzing and reflecting on it; and it is precisely this gesture, complemented, essential, with a Marxist sensibility and criticism, whether evident or latent, that provides opportunities to imagine and/or aestheticize reality and chances to realize and/or politicize the imagination without betraying both. About *MISS UNIVERSE*, that was the intention: to consider, decide, and invent an occasion in which, dialectically, femininity, capable and potentially disruptive, assuming its problems and its contradictions, rejecting its models and its patterns, would be articulated and exhibited in one of its many possible prefigurative forms of transgression and subversion. That was my job, solely and simply, nothing more and nothing less. For a bit of money, but above all for posturing and against bourgeois sensibilities.

M.U. I was free on Mondays and every morning because I worked at night. I don't know… I slept. Sometimes I wrote poems.

J. What kind of poems?

M.U. Sonnets. Just kidding. I don't know, I wrote poems. That's all.

J. Do you still write?

M.U. No, not anymore.

J. Do you have time for love? Are you in love?

M.U. You asked me about eroticism before. No, I don't have time for eroticism of the heart. I don't have time for love.

J. And what about sex? Do you have time for sex?

M.U. I have a bit more time for eroticism of the body, yes. But eroticism of the body seems boring and mechanical to me if eroticism of the heart doesn't happen, if it isn't introduced or extended.

J. Could you understand sex without love?

[follow on page 72]

An

 essay

by

The finance bros black leather lace-up flat. Erotic? It could be, I suppose, in a basic machismo kind of way. Worn by the straight-edged male product of Western patriarchy, its flatness signifies 'sensible', 'safe'. A key component of his uniform SEARCH FOR: [YouTube: *How to Look Like a Finance Bro*], the man in the polished flat does not seek to venture beyond convention; he is agreeable, enjoys rules. Unlike the uniforms of soldiers, police officers or mechanics, affiliated with physicality and getting dirty, the man who wears the ironed shirt and shapely flat is removed from the erotic in our culture. The systematic nature of his labour places him in a different realm to operational or manual labourers. The cleanness, streamlined form, and office-bound nature of his shoes lack eroticism due to their lack of danger. Leather by default, they fit the default man whose feet they hold. ‡

The black leather motorbike boot or thigh-high heel, on the other hand, possesses a certain eroticism that feels simultaneously primitive and advanced. Each of these boots contains risk: the heavy durability of the motorbike boot is designed to move through open space at speeds beyond that of the organic human. And the thigh-high heel requires its walker to maintain spacial awareness whilst elegantly performing and retaining strength and balance. Typically worn by the sex worker, it belongs to a perceptively 'body-less' minority whose labour is inherently risky. The experiences in which the motorbike and thigh-high leather boot are found offer a 'thrill'. They are niche, financially valuable, and thus may be deemed a 'luxury' - although their lack of comfort may speak to a luxury that moves beyond pleasure into discomfort and even pain. ‡

Despite this symbolism of discomfort, we can visualise the seductive animalism exuded by the wearers in motion. The leather is purposeful, a contraption that both protects and contains the human flesh beneath. We find leathery forms of protection devised by humans throughout history, stemming from our primitive survival instincts to hunt and kill. Despite the advanced and varied material options offered by contemporaneity, the skin of dead animals is still prime in our manufacturing of goods. In categorising the result of our primitive ways as 'luxury', we are fetishising the macabre nature of evolution and the human quest for superiority to the point of making it 'sexy'. The leather car or gym seat, for example, adds aesthetic value to the mechanisms they decorate whilst offering comfort by protecting our bodies from the metal structures on which we sit.

Attributing sex appeal to inanimate objects has much to do with the commodification of 'things' and 'experience' SEARCH FOR: [Google: *Marxist's Commodity Fetishism*], which began under capitalism. Perpetuated initially in post-war America, capitalism created a faux dream focused on materialism, possession and luxury living. This fetishistic culture has intensified by pop culture and the Internet into what can only be described as a 'hyper-luxurious' and 'hyper-sexy' lifestyle goal. We are told that 'to have' is to be successful, worthy. Capitalism's commodification of things transports us to a realm of 'what if'; the material seduction playing on our subconscious desires and innate need to be 'seen' and to 'belong'.

Cronenberg's 1996 film Crash SEARCH FOR: [Filmaffinity: *Crash*] critiques the culture of material seduction; the narrative follows a group of car-crash survivors, addictively replicating their trauma between flesh and machine as an erotic experience.

The movie's poster shows the lead female character's thigh in fishnet tights, bound in an industrial-looking black leather and metal contraption created to stabilise her leg following a car crash injury.

Taken from a scene in the film, the still is of an erotic encounter she shares with a male character as they turn each other on in the very thing that damaged her flesh: a car. Her sexual aliveness here contrasts with the aestheticisation of death, surrounded by materials derived from dead animal skin, labour, the metal frame resembling an industrial tool and pain, her broken leg and gashed flesh from the car crash. It is clear in this scene that there is pleasure in her pain as she re-enacts her trauma for sexual gratification – a common practice in the BDSM world.

Cronenberg's stylistic and conceptual choice to emulate this originally underground subculture was not exclusive to *Crash*, as the BDSM aesthetic permeated '90s pop culture. Cult movies and TV mimicked bondage wear in their characters' fashion choices: Barb Wire, Buffy the Vampire Slayer SEARCH FOR: [YouTube: *Buffy Leather & Vinyl Compilation*] and Xena the Warrior Princess all show lead females styled in what may have previously only existed within the confinement of the dominatrix's dungeon. Each of these characters fights for a living, their strength and aptitude for danger seemingly symbolised through clothing typically worn by a kink-related sex worker.

We've seen a resurgence of '90s fashion over the last few years, but the BDSM and sex worker aesthetic, in particular, has seeped into mainstream culture in a whole new way.

The PVC Pleaser heel, designed for strippers dancing on the pole, was spotted on several celebrities at the Met Gala this year and debuted within the high-fashion context by this century's 'ideal' Kim Kardashian in 2022 for her Marilyn Monroe look SEARCH FOR: [Google: *Kim Kardashian Met Gala 2020*], while at this year's Met, we saw Pleasers on the feet of Janelle Monáe and Doja Cat. Reportedly worn for their 'neutrality' and height, the act of repurposing the uniform of the erotic labourer (a minority demographic) to achieve a desirable look at an elitist event points to the fetishistic social culture we currently reside in.

Pleasers are structural workwear designed for movement and durational comfort in the confinement of a strip club; their purpose is to seductively *please*. The long heel elongates the leg, and the flesh of the foot can be seen through the strap as if wearing nothing at all. The foot is crammed tightly into a clear PVC layer in a way that seems to emulate animal flesh in clingfilm on the shelf of the supermarket meat section.

Preserved and packaged compactly for consumer appeal and efficiency, the transparency is a crucial component of organising each animal body part for human consumption. Heavy-duty PVC is often found at manual and service labour sites, including meat markets, butchers and hospitals. Associated with preservation, it has an eerily sterile quality to it: devoid of the dead, yet confronting death. ‡

The visual of man-made plastic suffocating the organic matter underneath resembles images of breath play in kink. Formally known as sexual or erotic asphyxiation, clingfilm, plastic bags or specially designed BDSM hoods are used to choke or limit the breath SEARCH FOR: [Imagefap.com: *asphyxiation*], supposedly surpassing pleasure and pain, into the sublime.

Where the bind of leather seems to protect humans in motion, suffocation seeks to create stillness, removing the ability to 'do' so that all that remains is to 'be'. A human that cannot 'do' is comparatively childlike, as without function, we are reduced to our simplest form.

Stillness, then, represents death and birth – or before birth, even. A default part of suffocation is the warmth and sweat produced as the human body temperature responds to the plastic around the skin, creating an incubator of sorts. These conditions could be comparable to the womb, the ultimate stage of regression. ‡

Kink relating to the early stages of our lives has been discussed in psychoanalysis throughout history, particularly by Freud. SEARCH FOR: [Google: *Freud's Seduction Theory*] He suggested that kinks develop in our adult sexual lives as a way of processing childhood trauma, though this has been much disputed since and even questioned by Freud himself. This theory could be deemed plausible if we consider the aforementioned kinks, but these scenarios are typically played out in private settings due to their sexual nature. Perhaps this 'privately coded' aesthetic has now penetrated mainstream culture due to the technological advancements in our hyper-surveilled, exhibitionist existence. This would feed into the human desire to be 'seen' that commodity culture captured so well... ‡

Another aesthetic trending in recent years touches on the tactility of bondage, simultaneously emulating an experimental imaginativeness associated with child's play. Made popular by former dominatrix and queen of the streets Julia Fox, this industrial-DIY look is created by repurposing materials typically used in construction work.

Restricted like an object, Fox was spotted in 2022 wearing a single length of silver duct tape around her bust. That same year, Balenciaga created a monstrously provocative 'BALENCIAGA' packing tape catsuit, worn by Kim K at Paris Fashion Week. Wrapped by hand, KK was bound so tight she struggled to walk, having to be manually cut out of it later. And judging from the tiny size of Fox's bikini tape top, the raw tape was applied directly to her body SEARCH FOR: [Google: *Julia Fox Tape Bra*], meaning the only way to undress would be by ripping it directly from her skin and nipples. These looks – ensuring bodily confinement, stillness, discomfort and pain – connect manual labour and physical work with a childlike approach to dressing; a stark contrast of regime vs freedom, pain vs pleasure and sterile vs messy. ‡

In some ways, using relatively cheap and readily available materials may seek to democratise fashion in the way that Dadaism declared found objects as art and punks accessorised with industrial chains. Stripped of hierarchical structures and materialistic culture, the concept of DIY almost reduces humanity to its most primitive form, the one that existed before world structures and capitalism instilled the social values we operate on today.

Julia Fox may hold the card of democracy – a former sex worker and migrant from a poor, broken home – but Kim K is the pinnacle of luxury in the 21st century. She is a testament to how wealth and power can assist in manufacturing the 'ultimate woman'; her life and body are so curated, so manufactured that she's almost cyborgian. SEARCH FOR: [Spotify: *Dispatches from the Kardashian Simulacrum*] The Kardashian clan represent the 'hyper-luxury' goal mentioned earlier; they are 'sexy under capitalism', so sexy it could be asexual.

Bondage combined with asexuality seems to negate any concept at all, and the act of high-fashion houses fetishising the tools of manual labourers, declaring them 'luxurious' and desirable, goes against the 'anti' ethos that Dadaism or punk established by repurposing materials. What, then, is our culture saying by declaring these materials as erotic and fetishising material affiliated with death and labour? ‡

Perhaps, like Cronenberg's Crash, which examined the eroticisation of machines in a poignant era of technological change (and thus cultural evolution) we are now examining the man-made materials created to assist humans in building society as it is in its current state; materials that have aided the mechanisms of modernity, industrial capitalism, late-capitalism and neoliberalism.

Obsessed with our own progress at the expense of Earth's natural resources, we now seem to be in a mode of decline. ‡

Ozziline

@mercedes666_2

In our primitive years, we had no choice but to utilise the skin of dead animals for furnishings, clothing and practical mechanisms. Parallel to the primitiveness of our sexual instincts, perhaps the eroticisation of dead animals draws on a raw animalism we innately possess? Using sex appeal as a way to commodify these assets triggers our primal urges: declaring animal skin as 'luxurious' makes us desire it more. Leather is the most commonly found skin. Solid and rigid in its structure, its permanence is akin to capitalism. Death, too, is permanent. It totally and wholly disarms a being into the ultimate mode of submission. This brings us back to the question of stillness, a state that occurs before and after life. The taut nature of leather replicates this, binding our limbs and restricting our ability to move freely. These parallels between trending materials and political-economic systems might suggest that we eroticise the social model in which we reside through our aesthetics. But what are we trying to say? What does it mean to dress 'still'? Are we exhausted –*have we been exhausted*– of being human in contemporary culture? The act of dressing in another creature's skin may be an attempt to go back to the beginning of humanity, a time when we were socially aligned with animals. But then, dressing for stillness alludes to a death wish – can we become 'dead' before our actual death by wearing 'death'? If so, is this an attempt to regain control of our distressingly inevitable fate? Or is it an optimistic approach to an afterlife where 'luxury' transports us to the sublime? ‡

The sublime is always tempting, and it is particularly seductive in a culture that insists on a fast-paced existence. In BDSM, the sublime is a common goal **SEARCH FOR: [Google: *Edmund Burke On the Sublime*]**, theoretically reached by surpassing pleasure and pain. Surpassing pain is a familiar aspect of contemporary culture, as our social systems force us to work to survive, pushing our bodies into unnatural states. Work, specifically manual labour, feels sadomasochistic in itself, though, as discussed, we have attempted to devise tools that alleviate some of that workplace pain. ‡

From an S&M perspective, of course, the tools and materials designed to assist human labour are erotic. In sadomasochistic play, the sadist dominates the masochist's body, using tools to inflict pain on them as they lie, submitting to it. This behaviour is comparable to the 'real life' dynamics in which labourers accept discomfort because those in power have made their labour mandatory. But like all modes of kink, it feels as if we 'in the real world' have reached our limit. We are at a 'still' point in time, a moment in which no new mechanisms or materials are needed to build our world. We have reached or, in fact, exceeded the amount of 'things' that would aid our evolution. ‡

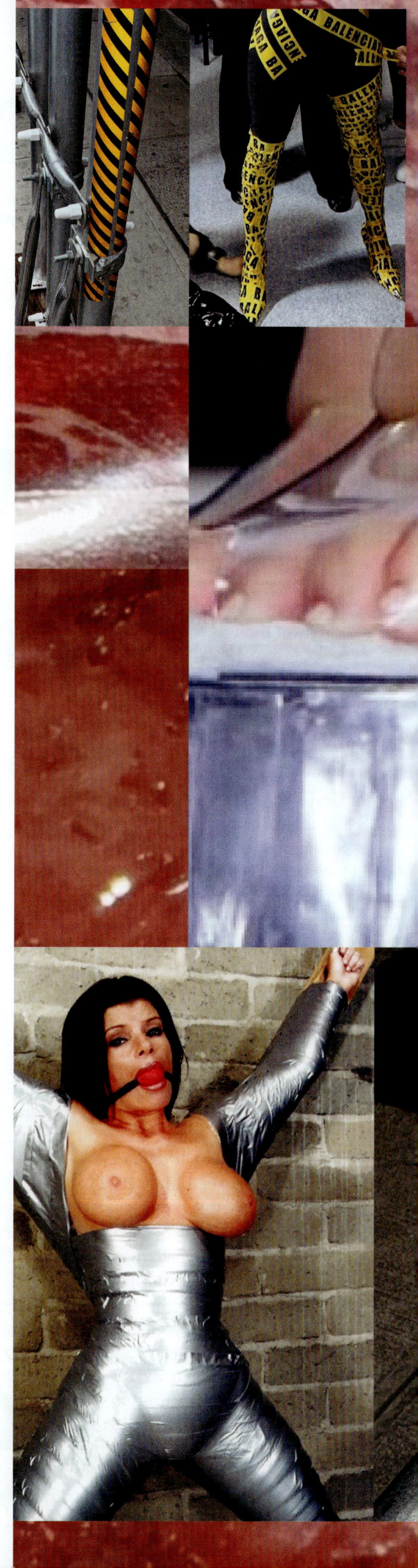

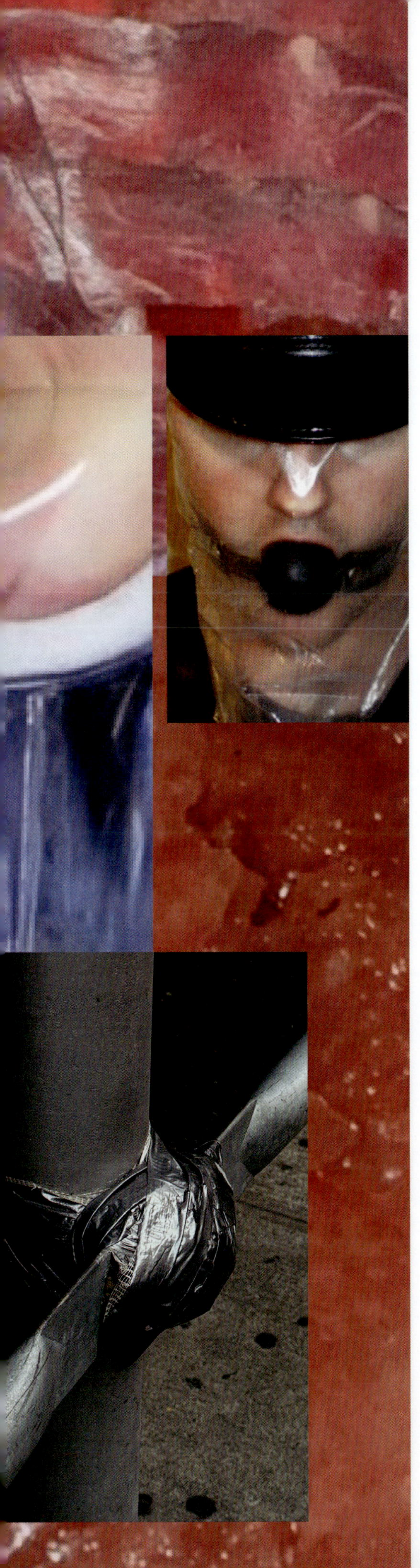

Our production limits have likely assisted in creating the DIY aesthetic, as we have moved into a neoliberal model that emphasises the 'self' over the possession of material goods. DIY aesthetics denote the value of 'clothing' by the wearer and label as opposed to the real money value of the materials used, their temporary nature embodying the liquid state of the neoliberal regime. SEARCH FOR: [Google Books: *Liquid Modernity by Zygmunt Bauman*]

But adopting materials typically used for jobs undertaken by the working classes and imbuing them with exclusivity and high value feels backwards in its appropriation: the uber-rich define their status by *wearing* these materials as opposed to using them for a functional task, thus conveying the message that 'your pain is my luxury'.

From this perspective, the incorporation of bondage into the DIY aesthetic makes a lot of sense. Kink is often about power dynamics, with specially designed items of clothing designated for the dominant or submissive role within the play. An appropriation of sorts also exists in kink, with humiliation being a popular request from submissive's, even if the 'submissive's' that enter the dungeon are often powerful outside it.

Being dominant in a dungeon with a submissive's consent is very different to the truths of a manual labourer with limited survival choices. The hard truth is that the globe's lack of wealth distribution has devastating effects on those with less, and this has possibly been more evident than ever in the last few years. ‡

So, are we really at the point of fetishising the wealth divide between the working class and the uber-rich? Is it now sexy to *own* your privilege? Are we repeating history? Will celebrities replace royals and aristocrats whilst the rest of us observe the gluttony with resentful aspiration? Pop culture's tendency to churn out nepo babies as the new It girl / model might suggest as much: Bella Hadid, Amelia Grey, Iris Law, Lily Rose-Depp, Kylie Jenner, Kim Kardashian, Paris Hilton.

Or if, on the other hand, DIY aesthetics aren't about power, could they be about symbolism? In her essay 'Against Ordinary Language: The Language of the Body ' DOWNLOAD: [Google: *YvonneBuchheim.com The Language of the Body PDF*], postmodernist writer Kathy Acker describes a physical 'language' experienced while training her body in the gym. She explains that 'the language of the body' rejects verbal description; that it is minimal and almost senseless. This approach might help us understand the stripped-down DIY aesthetic, as it is 'fashion' removed from what we know fashion to be. It is a concept, more than anything.

At the beginning of this essay, I suggested that uniforms relating to physical work are among the most fetishised items; the symbolism of these uniforms makes them what they are and makes us perceive their wearers in a certain way.

Collages by
Ozziline Mercedes

Images by
Ozziline Mercedes,
Imagefap and Instagram
@kimkardashian

Nowadays, 'work' does not hold the same specificity of aesthetics as it once did, as job roles do not contain the same clarity and we have moved away from rigid working conditions. Enabled through technology, neoliberalism made it all about the individual, and so for many of us, work consists of staring at screens in isolated rooms, still and silent.

The activeness and engagement of our bodies that came with farming or factory work pre-industrialisation has become vastly obsolete, yet, although this work contained a lot of pain and danger for the human body, there is a certain amount of fulfilment to be gained from physically exerting oneself.

As we sit in our comfortable bubble of self-curation, we likely crave the sense of community and physicality of our predecessors. Humans need to feel needed. It is good for our psyche to be put into roles, and as our sense of self is shaped by our surroundings, the role of every other human around us paradoxically creates a role for us. So, by wearing these materials, by eroticising 'work' in an aesthetic sense, are we asking to be made 'useful' again, as submissives ask of their dominant? ‡

We have moved through so many models of humanity, each new one a 'solution' to the problems of the last. Now, in our stillness, it appears that we have spiralled into a self-referential chamber of repetition, the only new solution to our destruction being regression – an undoing of the 'hyper' human condition. Is it possible that by finding the erotic in death and labour, we are provoking self-reflection on a mass scale? Our motivations could be comprehended through Acker's assessment of a 'bodily language' as formulaic; on the tearing and building of muscles in bodybuilding, she asks, "Is the equation between destruction and growth also a formula for art?".

In death and labour there is destruction. There is also growth. Is it possible, then, that in fetishising our own destruction, we are speaking a language that symbolises a truce between self and desires? A truce for humanity as we know it? Perhaps we have had to devise this language of aesthetics because the thing it must describe is beyond our verbal senses, beyond anything we have described before.

Luxury aesthetics have been redefined as minimal, the desirable as macabre: it seems we no longer get pleasure from the things we were once told we wanted the most, that we are redefining what it means to be human by dressing like a 'thing' – minimising our humanity with the intention of a simpler existence. It feels as though we have had enough. We have reached a post-pleasure era and moved beyond pain into a realm akin to sublimity, akin to death. ‡ ‡ ‡

APPRECIATING THE REMNANTS

I'm an artist and writer from County Wicklow, Ireland, working under the moniker Spicebag. I create work that interrogates Irish identity and politics. Ireland is the only post-colonial society in Europe; the tribalism and religious divides on the island go back centuries and fragment Irish identity. The cultural influences that drive my work stretch from paramilitaries to packets of crisps, unique signifiers of identity or symbols. Ireland has a national self-esteem issue; raped by its neighbour, it picks through the remnants of identity, putting together painful parts of itself during rehabilitation. We have to learn to speak again, learn to look people in the eye.

Being Irish is cool now – yuppies in London down pints of Guinness – but when my da was in London in the 80s, someone called the police when they heard him and his mate talking near a bank because they thought an IRA bombing was in progress. Irish people were treated like shit.

The island itself doesn't know whether it's coming or going; the regime bulimically discharges waves of its young people to work overseas, many never to return. Britain still occupies part of our homeland, and we've imported a culture war from America, hot on the heels of the very real 30-year conflict that ended the year I was born. House prices are the highest in the EU, as are rents and mortgages. Homelessness is at an all-time high and rioting and violence erupted across the capital. My identity and enchantment with my home and her people inform my work. Mise Eire. Appreciating the remnants, when there's no future, all you can do is look to the past, and that's what informs my work.

Slán agus Tiocfaidh ár lá.

MÁLA SPÍOSRAÍ

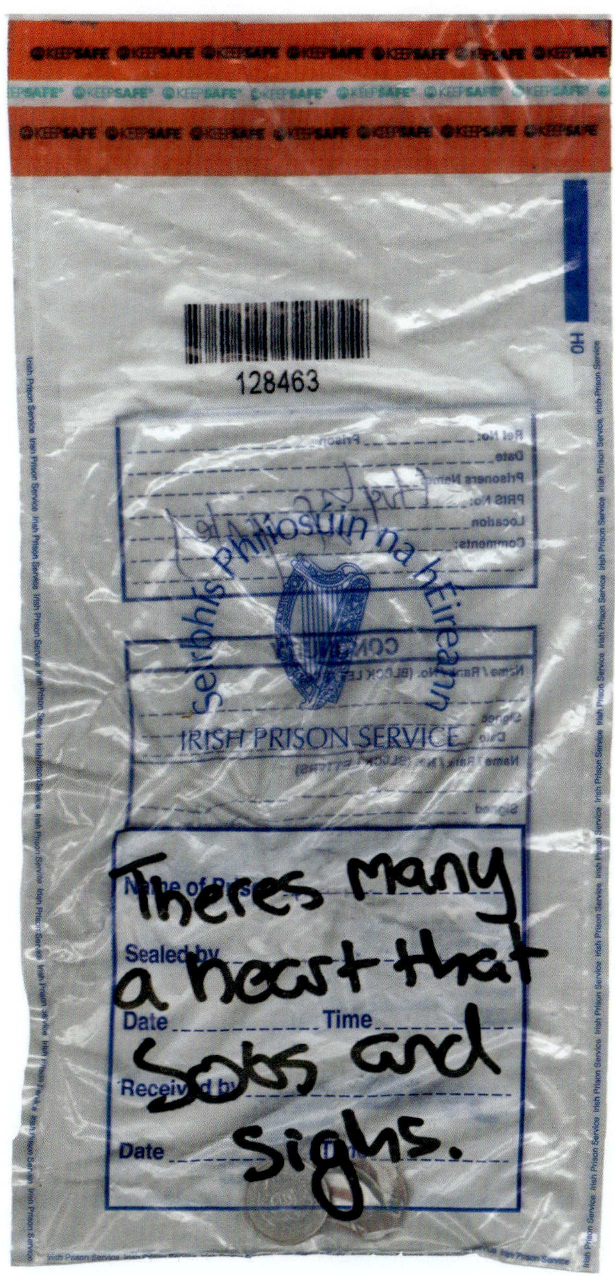

An ode to Irish Traveller musician Pecker Dunne.

Ecstasy tablets stamped with the logo of
An Garda Síochána – Ireland's national police force.

Ireland's most masculine symbol and cheapest pork product.

A bottle bong made from a Lourdes water bottle. When I was growing up, everyone's nanny had one of these in her house. Ireland was more or less a theocracy in the mid-twentieth century; now it is increasingly irreligious.

Part of an upcoming series called Tescocracy: imagining a centrally planned economy run by a supermarket conglomerate.

A piece highlighting the exploitation of loyalist youth
by loyalist paramilitaries in the north.

A work contrasting Ireland's current dystopian housing and rental landscape with the landlordism of the 1800s. This piece got national attention and resulted in a national debate around the eviction ban.

P R A D E E P

22

The pursuit of deep seabed mining amid a global climate crisis and ocean emergency

S I N G H

The mineral resources of the deep seabed have received increased attention in recent years. However, would mining the deep seabed truly result in a net benefit for humankind?

Pursuant to the UN Convention on the Law of the Sea 1982, the mineral resources in seabed areas beyond national jurisdiction ('the Area') are the common heritage of humankind. An intergovernmental organization, the International Seabed Authority (ISA), represents humankind as a whole in administering these resources. However, deep seabed mining (DSM) can also take place in areas within national jurisdiction, where coastal states have sovereign rights to explore and exploit the mineral resources within their jurisdiction.[1]

DSM refers to the extraction of minerals from the seabed at depths between 200 to 6.000 m. In more practical terms, the resources that are being targeted on the international seabed Area are found much deeper than 200 m: in some cases around 800 m and in other cases over 4.000 m. Three resource types are being targeted: polymetallic nodules (found at abyssal plains and is the deepest of the three resource types, typically between 3.000-5.000m), polymetallic sulphides (found at mid-ocean ridges and hydrothermal vent areas), and ferromanganese crusts (found at seamount areas). These deposits are known to contain significant levels of metals such as copper, nickel, cobalt, and manganese, among others.[2] These metals are the most sought-after globally in the commodities market, given their extensive use for electrical equipment, energy transmission and storage, construction, steel- and alloy-making, home appliances, and industrial machinery, among others.

Accessing each deep-sea resource type comes with its own set of challenges, some of which will be similar across the board while others could vary quite significantly.[3] First, the ecological setting is different among the three resource types (namely, abyssal plains, hydrothermal vents, and seamounts), therefore extraction activities would give rise to environmental problems that may differ in terms of type and scale. Second, and related to the previous point, is that different extraction methods would apply. For instance, remotely operated collectors using suction or vacuum technology would be deployed for the extraction of nodules, whereas drilling and cutting equipment will likely be used for the extraction of sulphides and crusts. Once collected from the seafloor, these minerals would be crushed and brought up to the vessel through a riser. Third, the onshore processing of these deposits may require different metallurgical processes, depending on the extracted ores and the type of metals that are targeted as commodities. Here, individual contractors would have to determine for themselves how and to where the extracted minerals would be transported for onshore processing. Irrespective of the resource type, it is anticipated that the entire extraction and refinement process would be highly energy intensive and time consuming.

On the one hand, proponents contend that DSM activities are essential to provide the metals that are necessary to combat climate change (e.g. to create batteries for electric vehicles and components for wind turbines) as well as to alleviate environmental pressures caused by terrestrial mining.[4] They assert that DSM activities are 'sustainable' and aligned with global political commitments such as the UN climate regime, the Paris Agreement, and the Sustainable Development Goals (SDGs). Under those agreements, states have committed to taking necessary steps to fight climate change and expedite the transition to renewable energy.

Another common argument made by DSM proponents is geopolitical.[5] They argue that a handful of countries –like Russia, but particularly China– have a very strong grip over certain commodities, and that for the world to depend on them to obtain these resources is undesirable and risky. However, it is noteworthy that the primary interest of DSM proponents to extract these resources is driven by individual economic interests and financial gains, and not to solve geopolitical tensions. In fact, the players that are leading the race for DSM are not big global players, and in some cases, are mere start-up companies. A few of them may have the backing of other bigger players that are established in the field of marine technology and engineering, but they do not have any particular experience with min-

1
The 1982 United Nations Convention on the Law of the Sea (see Parts VII and XI).

2
M. Lodge, 'The International Seabed Authority and Deep Seabed Mining', UN Chronicle, May 2017, https://www.un.org/en/chronicle/article/international-seabed-authority-and-deep-seabed-mining.

3
D. Jones, D. Amon and A. Chapman, 'Deep-Sea Mining: Processes and Impacts', in M. Baker, E. Ramirez-Llodra, and P. Tyler (eds) 'Natural Capital and Exploitation of the Deep Ocean'. Oxford University Press, 2020. ISBN: 9780198841654.

4
See for instance, The Metals Company, https://metals.co/products/.

5
The Economist, 'China is itching to mine the ocean floor', July 2024, https://www.economist.com/china/2024/07/28/china-is-itching-to-mine-the-ocean-floor.

ing for these mineral deposits (which is very different from offshore oil and gas extraction activities).[6]

On the other hand, critics argue that the green transition must be a clean and just one, while the immediate focus should be on designing a circular economy. Moreover, recent advances in marine sciences show that the deep ocean is rich in unique biodiversity and plays a pivotal role in regulating the global climate.[7] DSM could present a threat to the ecosystem functions of the marine environment, including to the marine food web and fisheries, although the potential scope and extent of such harm is still up for debate. Nevertheless, there is growing evidence to suggest that DSM will cause significant and irreversible harm to the marine environment, at least to the extent that it would be unwise and irresponsible to downplay or disregard the levels of such potential harm. Indeed, many local communities and indigenous people have voiced their concerns about DSM activities and how it may affect not only their livelihoods, but also their spiritual values and strong bond with the ocean.[8]

At the moment, it is also impractical to compare the effects of DSM with terrestrial mining, given that so little is understood about the deep-sea environment and the baseline information is scarce.[9] What we do know is that terrestrial mining activities usually involve operations that are targeted at certain specific sites that have a limited spatial extent, whereas the extraction of nodules under one single DSM operation will likely cover a significant area.[10] In any case, terrestrial mining is not going to stop or slow down if DSM happens. Rather, it is probably only going to increase in competition against DSM, if DSM does manage to become competitive.[11] Terrestrial miners are likely going to compete to ensure that they continue to have the edge, and they might even cut corners to do so. Consequently, opening up DSM could result in more terrestrial mining, thereby exacerbating effects like child labour or mining disasters. This also means that DSM will contribute very little to solving the current geopolitical struggles, and might even result in more competition, division, and distrust among the global powers.

Instead of DSM, countries can do so much more if they are serious about addressing our climate problem. They can invest a lot more in technology and research to find viable alternatives. For instance, there is now some interesting innovation in the batteries for electric vehicles, which can be developed better and stronger without cobalt. Countries can also embrace the concept of de-growth; namely that, as a society, we are living beyond our limits and the capacity of the planet to provide for us. This idea draws from the concepts of plenary boundaries and the limits to growth. Instead of perpetuating the business as usual mentality, we can collectively agree to do things differently. We also need to introduce more responsible terrestrial mining practices and find ways to secure the metals we may need through improved and sensible means, including through recycling but also through innovation to reduce the need for these metals. And such innovation is already happening, as mentioned earlier, with new batteries for electronic vehicles that do not require cobalt.

Yes, the deep seabed contains valuable minerals, including those that are sought for the clean energy transition. But, ultimately, is DSM our solution out of the climate crisis? It might not be the answer, and it is time to acknowledge that the pursuit of DSM would actually bury us further and deeper into the problem. Thus, claiming that DSM is necessary in our fight to reverse the climate crisis might be an overstatement. Our solutions to the climate crisis must be responsible ones, and it is clear that pursuing DSM today is irresponsible (considering the absence of a robust regulatory framework informed by science). This becomes more pertinent when we accept that we now find ourselves in an ocean crisis or emergency, with the ocean now facing unprecedented levels of threat due to human activities.

It is clear that the reason why governments are now taking serious action against climate change is largely due to pressure from youth and younger generations. If one were to ask the same youth activists that have been fighting for climate justice whether their proposed solution is DSM, the likely answer is a resounding no. If DSM proponents are indeed saying

6
For an overview of some of the main DSM players, see https://deepseamining.ac/companies#gsc.tab=0.

7
Ocean and Climate Platform, 'The deep sea: a key player to be protected for climate and ecosystems', https://ocean-climate.org/en/awareness/the-deep-sea-a-key-player-to-be-protected-for-climate-and-ecosystems/.

8
J. Hunter, P. Singh and J. Aguon, 'Broadening Common Heritage: Addressing Gaps in the Deep Sea Mining Regulatory Regime', Harvard Environmental Law Review, April 2018, https://journals.law.harvard.edu/elr/2018/04/16/broadening-common-heritage/.

9
A. Metaxas et al., 'Comparing environmental impacts of deep-seabed and land-based mining: A defensible framework', Global Change Biology, May 2024, Vol. 30, Issue 5, https://doi.org/10.1111/gcb.17334.

10
Planet Tracker, 'The sky high cost of deep sea mining', June 2023, https://planet-tracker.org/wp-content/uploads/2023/06/Deep-Sea-Mining.pdf.

11
P. Singh, Deep Seabed Mining and Sustainable Development Goal 14. In: W. Leal Filho, A.M. Azul, L. Brandli, A. Lange Salvia, and T. Wall (eds.) 'Life Below Water. Encyclopedia of the UN Sustainable Development Goals'. Springer, Cham, 2021. https://doi.org/10.1007/978-3-319-71064-8_135-1.

that DSM is for the future, why not ask the youth whether this is what they want when they call on governments to solve the climate crisis? This is important because the youth and the younger generations are the best suited to represent the interests of future generations.[12] DSM could threaten the rights and interests of future generations to a healthy and productive ocean, particularly given that the impacts of DSM using current technologies would cause irreversible environmental harm.[13]

Apart from the youth, scientists also play an important role in the debate. Scientists and experts should find ways to get involved and to contribute to the process, including by volunteering their time and expertise. Scientists can publish their research and present their findings to decision-makers, thereby helping to guide them in making more informed decisions. Civil society and other NGOs also play an important role by constantly applying pressure to government officials. Using their sphere of influence, these groups can demand answers and hold governments accountable for their failures. Similarly, indigenous groups should also be given the opportunity to convene and represent their views to decision-makers, including to stress their cultural and spiritual connection to the ocean, which would be further threatened by DSM. Finally, artists and educators should also be encouraged to contribute to the process, including by producing art, film, as well as syllabi with the aim to increase awareness and foster ocean literacy among the public.

As noted in a recent advisory opinion by the International Tribunal for the Law of the Sea,[14] governments have the obligation to protect and preserve the marine environment from all types of harm or threats to the ocean. This is particularly important given the climate crisis and ocean emergency we find ourselves in today. At the same time, states should fund more independent scientific research so we can better understand the deep sea, the extent of impacts that DSM will cause, and the benefits that we already receive and enjoy by sparing the ocean from DSM and avoiding the burdens therefrom. Only then can we take informed decisions about DSM, and we should postpone any rash decisions and refrain from allowing them to commence until then.

12
P. Singh, 'Deep seabed mining: 'For the benefit of humankind as a whole'?, RIFS Blog, May 2024, https://www.rifs-potsdam.de/en/blog/2024/05/deep-seabed-mining-benefit-humankind-whole.

13
Office of the UN High Commissioner for Human Rights, 'Key human rights considerations on the impacts of seabed mining', https://www.ohchr.org/sites/default/files/documents/issues/climatechange/information-materials/ohchr-seabed-mining-10-july.pdf.

14
ITLOS, Case No. 31, Advisory Opinion of 21 May 2024, https://www.itlos.org/fileadmin/itlos/documents/cases/31/Advisory_Opinion/C31_Adv_Op_21.05.2024_orig.pdf.

15
R. Sumaila et al. 'To engage in deep-sea mining or not to engage: what do full net cost analyses tell us?', *npj Ocean Sustain* 2023:2, 19. https://doi.org/10.1038/s44183-023-00030-w.

Countries and society as a whole must focus on responsible and equitable options in our fight to tackle the climate crisis and reverse current trends of loss of biodiversity and pollution. We should be cautious of solutions like DSM or marine geoengineering, which might cause more harm than good, even though they may sound promising initially. In our quest to restore balance with nature, we must leave out DSM until we have sufficient scientific information about its impacts and we are confident in our ability to manage them, as well as collectively agree to accept the burdens that come with DSM.[15] In conclusion, a proverb might be useful here to help relate to the dilemma at hand: we all need money to survive, but does that mean it is fair to rob a bank or steal from others?

HÉCTOR CASTILLO
BERTHIER

THE NECESSARY EVILS

STREET

+ VISUAL ESSAY +
KARLA READ

PIECES OF REALITY

n Mexico City there are countless failures, malfunctions, bsences, oversights, missions, and plenty f garbage thrown indiscriminately across he length and breadth f the streets and eighborhoods. These re pitiful "pieces f reality." In these laces we can see laws and deficiencies. We could designate hem as "spaces of ecessary evils." The mages and symbols hat accompany them speak to us about this. An aphorism says: Collective misery is flaunted as a continuation of progress", and within that "progress", poverty and indigence re a fundamental part f daily rituals... A ountry is governed y rituals. ▪ Let me xplain: the community often remedies he voids, deficiencies, and absences of uthority by itself, hrough "necessary vils" and their street ituals. ▪ Altars, virgins, saints, or death tself usually appear magically" in the middle of the streets and venues to solve several unsettled problems: garbage, paving, traffic, street commerce, nd many others (born rom informality—often legitimized by he neighbors themselves—). They seek to xercise power at the ocal level with different representations: the power of nooks nd street altars"; the sanctuaries that manate from the eighborhood and its eople"; "the symbols

ALTARS

that are born to obtain the respect of the masses"; and that end up acquiring a social recognition that frequently supplants institutional functions… The altars rule. The reality of the myth is part of the unreality of the country. ▪ When did the capital cease to be "The City of Palaces" and became an endless, insufferable, violent, dirty Metropolitan Zone, so full of graffiti and diverse images and symbols? ▪ The city is a zone full of failings. And today, that territory is devouring itself. And amid its body and its tissues appear numerous images to rediscover, reinterpret, and recognize a new city, suspicious, violent, sheltered, protected, whose daily inhabitants circulate and coincide—or disagree. ▪ The inner-city and marginal areas are characterized by poverty-stricken housing, and, in several sectors, there are neighborhoods in precarious conditions. That is to say, they barely meet the basic elements to be habitable, but they are already immersed in all the urban problems of the most lacking districts of the city. ▪ In these places –as in most places of this kind–, various problems are present on a daily basis: corruption, destitution, prostitution, dilapidated housing, social disorder, vandalism, illegal spaces, out-of-control street vendors, street encroachment, congestion, road disorder, and many more.

I AM AN OPTIMIST: LONG LIVE RITUAL!

Nevertheless: "We are a ritual people. And this tendency benefits our imagination as much as our sensibility, always tuned and awake", wrote Octavio Paz in his *Labyrinth of Solitude* (Ed. FCE, 1960). And there are some concepts to understand its importance today. ▪ This ritualism is expressed in our calendar, full of feasts and celebrations, from the most remote places to the big cities. People eat, get drunk, pray, shout, dance, sing and celebrate, perhaps to better endure the hardships of the whole year. But not just the feasts are ritualized; the necessary evils, the problems, are also ritualized. Social resentment begins at home. ▪ Our poverty can be measured by the sumptuousness and number of our popular festivals, but our ills and troubles can also be gauged by the multiplicity of altars and shrines that appear scattered across popular neighborhoods. Altars and shrines are a ritual expense of the community, hoping that they will prove useful to it… in some way. ▪ Urban space always opens in the mind to know, discover, interpret, or analyze the city on an imaginary backdrop. As if it were a canvas for a painting. ▪ It is true. In many streets, images of the Virgin of Guadalupe are recreated in the hopes

that, with her appearance, the clandestine garbage dumps will be eliminated. However, there are many other figures and representations. ▪ For example, the symbols of death appear. Life is prolonged in death. Death is not the natural end of life, but a phase of an infinite cycle. Life, death, resurrection were stages of a cosmic process that repeated itself insatiably. Life had no higher function than to lead to death, its opposite and complement; and death, in turn, was not an end in itself. Religion and Destiny governed life, just as morality and freedom preside over ours. ▪ Today, modern death has no significance that transcends it or refers to other values. In almost all cases it is — simply—the inevitable end of a natural process. ▪ Death is: Holy, beautiful, beloved, light, night, black, bony, companion, final kiss, last breath… But she's a tough one when she comes.

THE WHITE GIRL (SANTA MUERTE)

In a showcase placed at the gate of the Parish of Mercy, located in the central Colonia Morelos in Mexico City, a life-size, elegantly and ornately clothed Holy White Girl (as believers also call her) displays her scythe while holding the world on the palm of her left hand. ▪ At the back of the building –which used to be an early 20th century house– stands the main altar of the Sovereign Lady, where hundreds of people come every week to pray to or to ask for favors. ▪ Among flowers and candles, at least 20 images and pictures of the "Mighty Lady" make up the altar where her devotees offer her red apples, water, white bread, incense, and even leave her cigars, which –as per to the belief– must always come in pairs, one for her and one for the devotee. ▪ In *La Santa Muerte* (Ed. Debolsillo, 2017), Homero Aridjis investigates the recently-known expressions of creativity about the inexhaustible Mexican religious syncretism, and, without deviating from his literary goals, analyzes the social aspects of the cult of death. ▪ "It is a very strong cult that is on the rise, it is linked to the Day of the Dead tradition, it has historical roots both in pre-Hispanic times and in the Colony, and it fits very well with contemporary Mexico", he says.

That image we had of death, sinister, painful, cruel and cold, has evolved with our own mentality. At last, we have discovered that this personification serves to prepare us for the last moment of our earthly existence, to reach a level in which our conscience, thought, and intuition are at peace so we may transcend to the region of its dominions and, later, to a superior one of Supreme character. ▪ Currently, Santa Muerte endures and is worshipped in multiple altars where "ceremonies" (masses) are celebrated on Sundays or on dates chosen by each church. In those places, her faithful followers —who acknowledge each other as "little brothers"— devote to her this prayer, among many others: "*In the name of the Father, of the Son, and of the Holy Spirit, immaculate being of light, I implore you to grant me the favors I ask of you, until the last day, hour, and moment in which your Divine Majesty orders to have me taken me to your presence. Dear Death of my heart, do not forsake me with your protection.*"

ST. JUDE THADDAEUS

One more image. Every 28th of every month, thousands and thousands of visitors pay tribute and honor to one of the most popular saints today, St. Jude Thaddaeus, in the temple of St. Hippolytus, where this "saint" is located and which is said to be very miraculous. ▪ The temple of St. Hippolytus was built by the conquistadors to remember the day they succeeded in taking over Mexico City, on Tuesday, August 13, 1521, on the feast of the saint in question. ▪ The temple of St. Hippolytus is located on Tacuba road, where the brave Mexicas struck the Spanish army "even underneath their tongues" during the events of the so-called "Noche Triste" (Sad Night) of June 30, 1520. ▪ It was in this area where a Spanish soldier, Juan Garrido, decided to build a shrine in memory of the fallen conquistadors. It was initially called "of the martyrs." Garrido set out to collect the remains of his dead comrades to give them a Christian burial in the shrine. ▪ Vicente Riva Palacio, in his work *México a través de los siglos* (Ed. Espasa y Ballescá, 1884), estimates that more than half of the Spanish soldiers perished in battle, which by then –counting the armies of Hernán Cortés, Pedro de Alvarado and Pánfilo de Narváez– totaled

1,600 Spaniards and 7,000 Indians. ▪ The founding of any city in America was always accompanied by the designation of a celestial patron who, the new settlers thought, would intercede for them. In its viceregal stage, Mexico City had several patron saints that transformed over time, and St. Hippolytus, whose feast is on August 13, was the first of them. ▪ So as not to forget, let me tell you that religious and civil celebrations were mixed with each other in these spaces. Religious festivities fulfilled their function of strengthening the people's belief in the Catholic Church. The civil ones had propagandistic goals in favor of the interests of the ruling classes and the oligarchies, and also served to renew the obedience and loyalty of the subjects to the King of Spain, regardless of the thousands of kilometers that separated them in presence. History is the only domain where impunity does not rule. ▪ Although the church of St. Hippolytus was dedicated to the first patron saint of Mexico City, today it is much better known by the peculiar devotees of St. Jude Thaddaeus, who flock to it on a massive and ever-increasing scale.

St. Jude Thaddaeus is known as the saint of “impossible causes”, to whom the following prayer is dedicated: “ *“I come before you with all the faith in my soul to seek your sacred solace in my difficult situation; do not forsake me at the doors that are to open in my path, may your powerful arm be the one to open them in what I so yearn for* (here, one must make three wishes that are difficult to fulfill), *this supplication comes from a heart afflicted by the hard blows of cruel destiny, which have defeated him always in the human struggle, since, if your divine power were not to intercede in my favor, I will perish due to lack of help. Mighty arm of my good Jesus, assist me, protect me, and grant me heavenly glory.”* ▪ St. Jude Thaddaeus is the favorite saint of policemen, prisoners, ex-prisoners, and relatives of prisoners. In the church of St. Hippolytus, on the 28th of each month, it is easy to find *acholado* rappers, MC Luka style. A great many *cholos* attend, all very similar to the terrifying characters that the TV (the “idiot box”) sells us when it talks about the famous “Maras” –the “Salvatrucha”, “la 13”, “la 18”, the “Mexican Mafia”, etc. ▪ In the Juvenile Protection Council, detained youths rigorously weave scapulars with the image of St. Jude Thaddaeus, and when

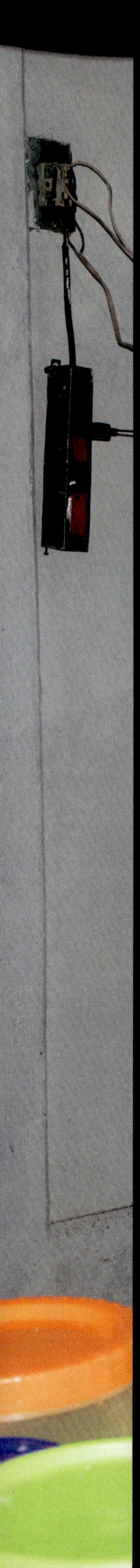

they get out, they go to the church to give thanks, and then they bring the whole family with them. ▪ The cult of St. Jude Thaddaeus is very similar to that of Santa Muerte; however, it is obvious that it really "pulls" in mostly young people and children, while Santa Muerte gathers many more adults. ▪ So many people go to St. Hippolytus on the 28th that the police have to cordon off the area to manage the entrance and exit of the people. In attendance is a lot of *banda*, lots of crews, a lot of hood, "*pura bandota chida*", though the *banda* scares off the adults and many of the kids are seen huffing into burlaps drenched in thinner and solvents. ▪ "*San Juditas*, powerful arm of the good 'Chuy', don't allow the ineptitude of our policemen to keep massacring the kids", a street altar read.

COLOPHON

The history of necessary evils is common and frequent, very similar to the development and growth of many other spaces of the city. Regardless of when the first inhabitants arrived to the neighborhoods, the conditions of poverty and marginality persist. What's worse: many of their habits and forms of survival have been adapted and accepted as "necessary evils" that will not only continue to be reproduced on a daily basis, but will end up being seen as something natural by them.

The list of problems that exist can be explained by many other mechanisms of "disorder", "corruption" or "absent government" that are always present. The existence of the *tianguis* is a magnificent example of this. In these popular street markets, you can find almost anything, from a luxurious *quinceañera* dress to the illegal sale of weapons and drugs.

Today, these places are no longer on the periphery; they are in the center of municipalities and increasingly appearing in the new housing developments (or very close to them) with new inhabitants who are probably unaware of these practices.

We all suffer the consequences of street vending. There is not a single place that has not been invaded by these businesses. For a long time, there has been talk of "controlling", "preventing", "impeding", "relocating" or, straight up "disappearing" informal commerce.

Nothing has worked, and there are so many economic and political interests behind it, that it seems very difficult to really achieve a reorganization of street vending and the problems it brings with it.

It is not easy to predict the future. However –as has been mentioned–, the "evils" will continue to be "necessary". With them, we could create a sample display of the problems that are born, reproduce, and will be reborn, since –surely– they will reproduce permanently in many other parts of the country.

"It is a pity that each government takes six years to learn what happened in its six-year term", as Carlos Monsiváis would have said. Everything changes, everything is transformed... so that everything remains the same, or worse.

OBJECTS AT THE END OF LOVE:

by Ania

PERFORMING SADNESS WITH THINGS

POST-LOVE CLUTTER

When love ends, there is clutter –objects collected throughout the relationship. Once the love is over, these items transform into memorabilia, producing a shift in the meaning and role wherein sadness emerges. This shift is also where grieving begins to take on a positive momentum. Therefore, being the symbols of sadness, objects of lost love serve a distinct and distinctly performative function. Not only do they redefine our status (shifting from *loved* or *in love* to *abandoned*, *left*, *stuck*, *detached*, etc.), but they also influence how we engage with love experiences –both past and future.

GRIEF WORK

Sadness –as focused on the present moment– reflects our immediate relationship with the world by constantly assessing how we cope with the loss of a loved one (Granek 2010, 49). Thus, objects of lost love provide a paradoxical cure: they can contaminate our psyche yet help us navigate melancholia. Sadness is a natural response to loss. It is also a natural trigger of what Abraham (1927) calls "grief work" –a process of reconceptualisation and revelation. In this process, sorrow is not just accumulation but also a necessary commotion that, as Deutsch (1937) observes, must be fully experienced to the point of exhaustion.

TRANSFER OF MEANING

The items of love, having become the props of loss, exhaust grief through the transfer of meaning. Transferring despair and loneliness onto the objects once associated with a loving bond redefines that bond according to its new status and produces a powerful coping mechanism. This helps deactivate the experience of love by activating commemoration through tangible reminders. As objects imbued with specific emotional context, these reminders allow us to express sadness fully and prevent the grieving process from hindering. They also re-associate emotionally charged memories to give sadness a new anchor.

FALLING FOR THINGS

The key aspect of grieving lost love with objects is a realisation that the feelings and experiences of love are mostly about "things". Even the *love object* (the person we love) eventually appears to be the *sum total* of the "items" we miss and fell for in the first place. In psychological terms, to be in love is to project an ideal onto a person based on the attributes of appeal. The person as such is often irrelevant. What is relevant, though, is the props we associate with the fantasy of the ideal, and those props invariably satisfy. Falling in love is not falling for people; it is falling for items filled with meaning about those people. Love is never in the essence but always in the matter, and the entire practice of love is founded

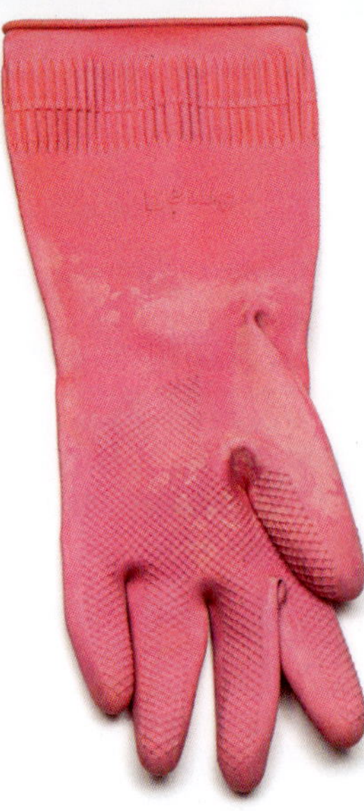

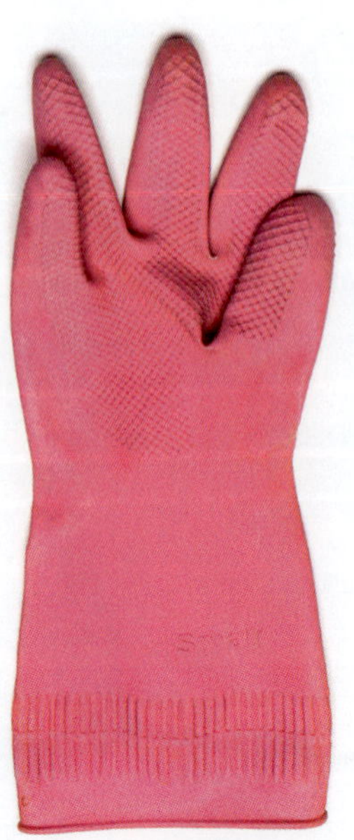

on things (attributes, gestures, actual objects) –their exchange, accumulation and collection.

OBJECT POWER

In *Love Objects. Emotion, Design and Material Culture*, authors Anna Moran, Sorcha O'Brien and others examine "the emotional potency of objects", showing "how objects can become symbols and representations, as well as active participants in and mediators of our relationships with each other" (2014, xiv). The intimate stories of things and people they share (including the stories of wedding tableware, love letters, gift articles, jewellery and other items intersecting with affection or desire) reveal that "objects engage our emotions subliminally, viscerally and vicariously [by] serving as intentional bearers of significance through embodiment, engagement or control" (ibid). The role of objects in transitioning past lost love is to "provide security and symbolic connection with valued others when separated from them" (Goldstein et al. 2020). It is also to re-orient the environment, which, once home to that love, now displays abandonment.

REDECORATION

Roland Barthes (1977), who considered love the constellation of things in time, space and context, observes that items that came between people in love were the extensions of the event of love they experienced. "Every object touched by the loved being's body becomes part of that body, and the subject eagerly attaches himself to it" (173). When love lasts, "the metonymic object is a presence (engendering joy)"; when love ends, "it is an absence (engendering distress)" (173). The sadness of love is, therefore, not as much a feeling but a landscape brimming with void. Items that once informed appearance suddenly inform lack. Dealing with lost love involves dealing with the entire environment in which love occurred and where the objects that once represented it now fail to express the new emotional organisation. That is why, perhaps, enduring the sadness of lost love takes a lot of *redecoration*.

LOST LOVE ON DISPLAY

There are many ways to redecorate feelings: ritualistic, private, communal and others. One of them is display. In 2006, Olinka Vištica and Dražen Grubisic started the Museum of Broken Relationships –a repository of post-love objects from donors willing to redecorate their grief and show it to the public. The museum was first conceived as "an installation at a local art festival" (Vištica and Grubisic 2017, 6), but with time, it became one of Croatia's most emblematic art attractions and a one-of-a-kind international phenomenon, gathering over four thousand "objects of love wreckage" (ibid), of which some seventy were exhibited in the museum's gallery space.

All images courtesy of the Museum of Broken Relationships

Previously split between locations in Zagreb and Los Angeles (the former opened in 2010 and is still operational), the museum followed Vištica and Grubisic's own break-up that had left them torn between mutually shared possessions, many of which they neither wanted to keep nor give up. The immediate question to support their dilemma was: "What can one do with the frail ruins of a love affair?" (Vištica and Grubisic 2017, 6).

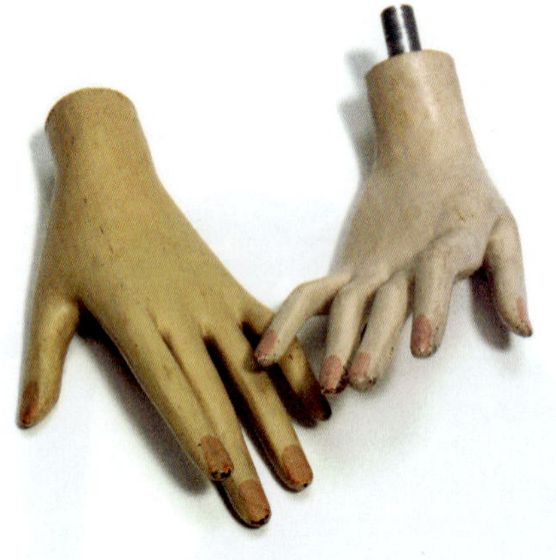

EMOTIONAL REPOSITORY

The Museum of Broken Relationships answers the question of *love remnants in keepsakes* with an encouraging call on its website (www.brokenships.com): "Recently ended a relationship? Wish to unburden the emotional load by erasing everything that reminds you of that painful experience? Don't –one day, you may regret it. Instead, send your item to our museum and take part in the creation of a collective emotional history" (The Museum of Broken Relationships website). Donations are handled physically (objects are provided by traditional mail) or digitally (images of objects are shared in the website's dedicated tab). These methods of building a collective story of unhappy endings show a deep understanding of the universality of lost love –further illustrated by the locations of donated objects mapped on the museum's website and noted in the object descriptions. This mass contribution shows that broken relationships are a global matter of various conditions. They occur widely, regardless of geography and cultural influences; and they entail millions of people –practically everybody, in fact.

MATTERS OF SADNESS

The museum has four layers: the objects, the contexts (histories/stories and people behind the objects), the donations, and the expositions. All represent different shades of sadness, carefully tended by Charlotte Fuentes –the museum's manager– who curates them for permanent and temporary shows and keeps the memory of love and grief alive. The items in the collection (on display and in the depository) form emotionally themed constellations. Each one renders a sadness regarding the situational, intentional or relational dimensions of a given relationship. Most common are *effigies* (e.g. "Porcelain figures" from Dublin, Ireland), *tissues* (e.g. "Lock of hair" from Mexico City, Mexico), *wearables* ("Garter belt" from Sarajevo, Bosnia and Herzegovina), *utensils* ("Ceramic rolling pin" donated from Bedford, UK), *souvenirs* ("Postcard" donated from Yerevan, Armenia), *media* ("GPS" donated from Tempe, AZ, USA), and *abstracts of daily care* ("Pencivir herpes cream from Cologne, Germany). There are also recycles, such as a piñata made from love letters (New York and Los Angeles, USA) or "Wedding dress in a jar" from San Francisco, CA, USA, whose background story explains the item creation: "We were together for seven years, five of them married. Our wedding was a small casual ceremony near the ocean on the island where we lived. I wore a silk dress covered in butterflies and flowers that I always thought I'd wear again but never did. He's been gone a year now, and I haven't really known what to do with that dress. [...] I put it in this jar because [...] it's a lot less sad when it's not hanging empty on a hanger" (Vištica and Grubisic 2017, 10).

MATERIAL REALISATIONS OF FEELING

Other similar stories account for the nature of longing, disappointment, anger, nostalgia and melancholia released by the broken relationship objects. An insight into the circumstances of those stories unravels different sub-affects of sadness that each of the objects ensues. "Before he left to join the Peace Corps, he bought me a car and gave me his GPS so I wouldn't get lost" (Vištica and Grubisic 2017, 143), says the story of a media device once symbolising thoughtful concern. "He got these shoes for me at a sex shop in Pigalle" (ibid, 152) informs a tale of a pair of red stilettos, once a token of intimacy, passion, sexual language and connection the couple shared. Stories of care, like the story of the acupuncture pens given to a partner to help them cope with constant illness, render traces of tender investment. There are also stories of the mundane: everydayness once experienced and enjoyed and now reduced to materials of commemoration, like a collection of used contact lenses saved by a partner over three years from their bedside. The most poignant, however, are the stories of regret: "It was three hundred days too long. He gave me his mobile phone so I couldn't call him anymore" (Vištica and Grubisic 2017, 91). They are counterbalanced by accounts of gratitude, like the story of a donor of a bracelet (a reminder of a holiday at Disney World): "Thank you for all the lessons you taught me and the strength you left me with, without even realising it" (ibid, 164).

CONSERVATION OF COLLECTIVE PAIN

Transforming the objects of broken relationships into a testimony of sadness for the love that was there –something the Museum of Broken Relationships invariably does– subscribes to a more universal mission: to capture fleeting relationships between people and things. It also supports the preservation of performances emerging from ordinary interactions with objects: their feelings, affects, states and functions. There is also the collective aspect, in that when experienced collectively and individually, these operations bring the sadness of love to full affirmation. They also reveal the reason we imbue objects with sadness and why we need to affirm the sadness at the end of love: the acknowledgement of pain achieved through preservation and display. As such, the objects become a source of pleasure or, to be precise, a source of closure, producing "a kind of strange sadness": a paradox expressed by John Hospers, who said, "Sad experiences, such as suffering, personal loss, bereavement or keen disappointment, are not the kind of thing we wish to repeat or prolong. Yet [this repetition in representation] may bring relief, pleasure, even happiness –a strange kind of sadness that brings pleasure" (1955, 326). That pleasure –one that disorients the sadness of lost love with objects– leaves loss objectively re-signified: open to new meanings and new en/de-coding(s). We need this to endure the impossibility of understanding sadness as a state and performative occurrence, just as we need to relive the material symbols of a relationship and the sadness. Why? To fully embrace "Whatever bears upon the question of 'how to *love*'" (cf. Arnold 1924, 143).

REFERENCES

Abraham, Karl. 1927. 'A short study of the development of the libido, viewed in the light of mental disorders'. In *Selected Papers of Karl Abraham MD*, edited by Douglas Bryan and Alix Strachey. Hogarth Press.

Arnold, Matthew. 1924. *Essays in Criticism*, vol.2. Macmillan.

Barthes, Roland. 1977. *A Lover's Discourse. Fragments.*, Penguin Books.

Deutsch, Helene. 1937. 'Absence of grief.'. *Psychoanalytic Quarterly* 6: 12–22.

Goldstein, Richard D., Carter R. Petty, Sue E. Morris, Melanie Human, Hein Odendaal, Amy J. Elliott, Deborah Tobacco, Jyoti Angal, Lucy Brink, and Holly G. Prigerson. 2020. 'Transitional objects of grief.'. *Comprehensive Psychiatry* 98: 152161. https://doi.org/10.1016/j.comppsych.2020.152161.

Granek, Leeat. 2010. 'Grief as pathology. The evolution of grief theory in psychology from Freud to the present.' *History of Psychology* 13 (1): 46–73.

Hospers, John. 1955. 'The concept of artistic expression.', *Proceedings of the Aristotelian Society, New Series*, 55 (1954/1955): 313–344.

Moran, Anna and Sorcha O'Brien. 2014. *Love Objects. Emotion, Design and Material Culture*. Bloomsbury.

Vištica, Olinka and Dražen Grubisic., 2017. *The Museum of Modern Relationships. Modern Love in 203 Everyday Objects*. Orion.

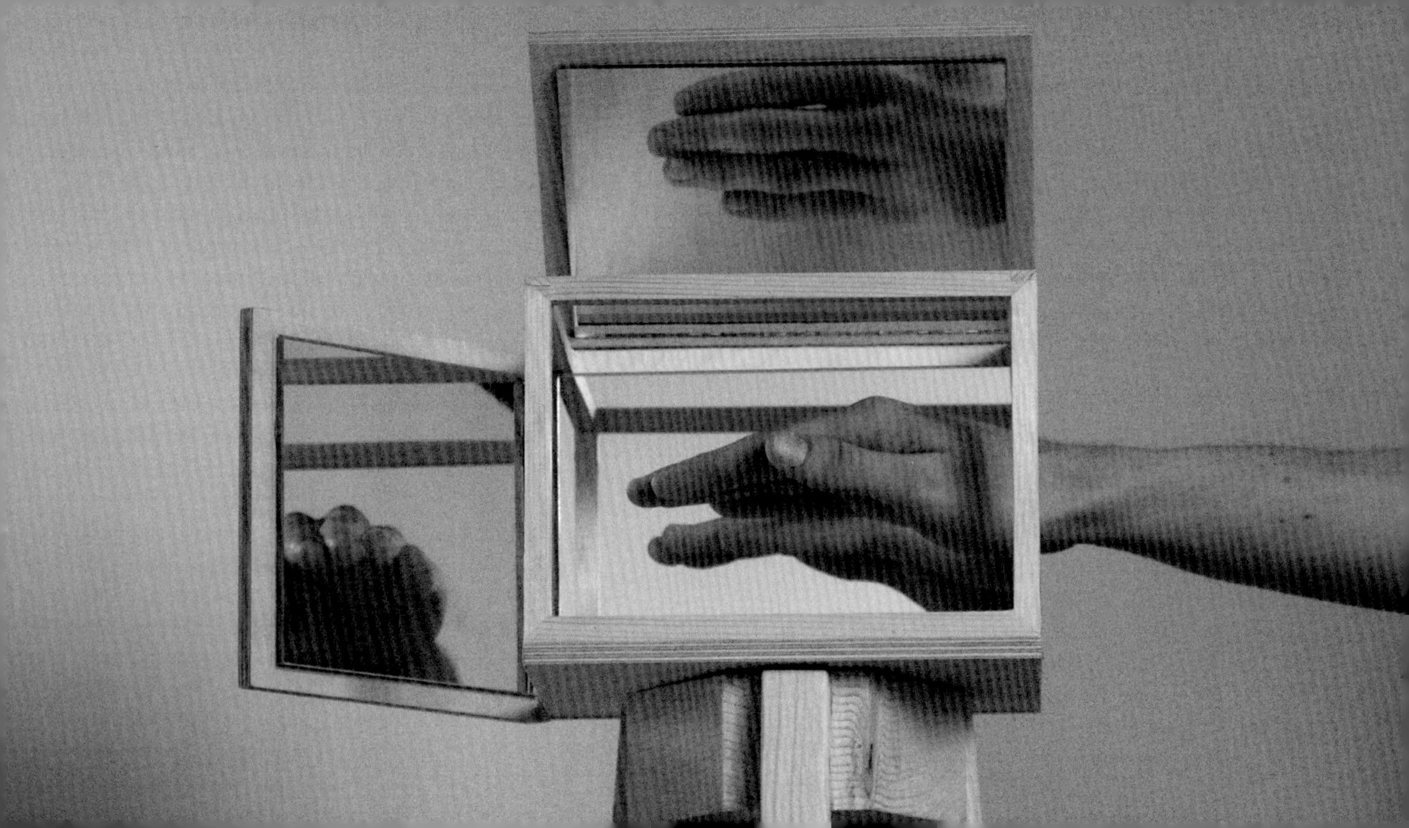

The Right-Handed Dictator

Ted Hyunhak Yoon

This essay can be seen as an effort to somehow deal with the loose connections that have emerged through my work on statues of dictators.

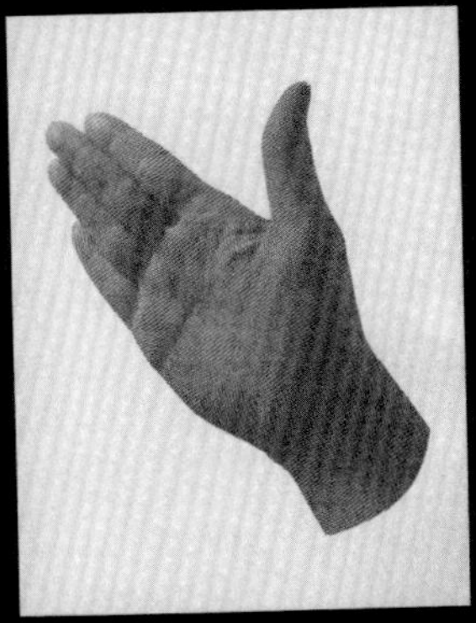

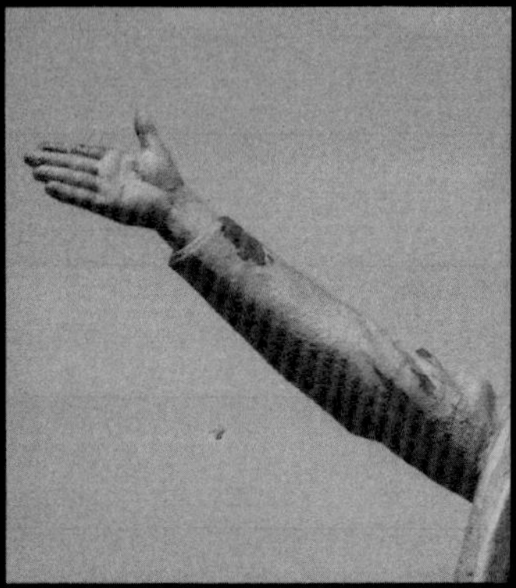

Part 1: Statues

My research emerged from a 2014 project called *Decoding Dictatorial Statues*, conducted during the RDP (research, design, publish) class at the Royal College of Art in London. It all started when I came across a 2011 article about some Koreans in Berlin who wanted to put up a statue of President Park Chung-hee, South Korea's longest-ruling dictator. This group, called Gluck Auf, was made up of Korean miners that Park Chung-hee had sent to Germany from 1963 to 1977. Their way of showing respect to him caused quite a controversy among other Koreans in Germany and back in South Korea. For many, building statues to honour specific figures felt pretty outdated and unfamiliar. From there, I continued to observe statues of dictators such as Lenin, Mao Zedong, and North Korea's Kim Il-sung and Kim Jong-il.

All images on this article are a recomposition of the image research from *Decoding Dictatorial Statues* (Onomatopee, 2019), unless stated otherwise

Why do people find statues of dictators controversial? In order to answer that question, my research was divided into two main axes: one dealing with the visual clichés of statues, which began at the project's inception, and the other addressing the existence and meaning of statues themselves through diverse social events triggered by their erection and dismantling. I collected images of statues from former Soviet states, North Korea and China, among others, focusing on how statues establish political images. Aside from historical and political contexts, could the visual characteristics of a statue make it a subject of controversy or convey specific images and messages to people?

A monument
of Park Chung-hee
(Indieplug, Danew Film)

Johan Maurits van Nassau-Siegen

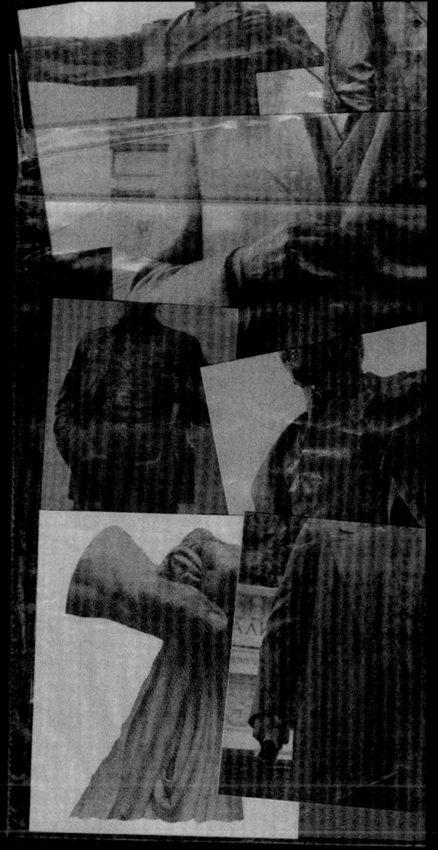

Following the classification of the gestures observed in statues of dictators, the project evolved into a book. Firstly, I focused on collecting images of statues of leaders who executed dictatorial governance in representative communist countries, observing the repetitive occurrence of visual similarities. I defined the act of viewing and analysing statues as "decoding". Secondly, I invited a group of decoders (including myself and other researchers) to share diverse stories relating to the contemporary phenomena surrounding these statues, such as the media's coverage of the iconoclastic images of the destruction of Saddam Hussein's statue in Iraq, the remains of Stalin's statue now on display in a theme park and zoo in Lithuania, or North Korea's production of statues for African states as part of their diplomatic efforts, such as the ones erected in Benin, Botswana, the Democratic Republic of the Congo, Mozambique, Ethiopia, Angola and Zimbabwe. By addressing statues across different times and places, the project examined how political statues in the public arena can serve as a node for diverse forms of power, communication and meaning.

Part 2: Statues - Oratory Gestures

Fig. 5.
Illustration on p.40,
A Manual of Gesture (1875)
by Albert Bacon

When describing gestures that seem frozen in time, I often used the term "a frozen moment". My curiosity extended to what kind of live gestures preceded a raised-right-hand pose before it was rendered into a statue. My next project was called "Notes on Gestures". While working on *Decoding Dictatorial Statues*, I spent a considerable amount of time contemplating statues, wondering why is that statue striking that particular pose and under what circumstances did it come to assume it? When delivering a speech, gestures play an essential role alongside the voice (sound), forming an integral part of the art of rhetoric. The domain of oratory or rhetorical gestures is meticulously documented in two significant texts: Albert Bacon's *A Manual of Gesture* (1875), which includes a "notation system for gestures"(noted for its heavy referencing of Gilbert Austin's *Chironomia*), and François Delsarte's *System of Oratory* (1893). An intriguing aspect of mastering the gestures is the existence of coordinates used for learning records. In Albert Bacon's *A Manual of Gesture*, illustrations featuring spherical coordinates provide hypothetical grounds for the meanings behind the gestures observed in statues. The graphics depicting these systems expanded my learning in the realm of gestures, providing new dimensions unseen in the earlier *Decoding Dictatorial Statues* project. Reworking Bacon's manual I sought to recompose its graphics. Consequently, I restructured the content from these texts into posters and transformed the practical elements of the book into performable pieces. This approach aimed to transcend my archetypal forms of production as a graphic designer. I translated the textual content into a performative manual where the process of embodying the gestures is performed in harmony with narrated indications. This juxtaposition was an invitation to reconsider how the hands, body movements and gestures of past and present-day politicians have influenced public perception.

Fig. 5.

LESSON IV.

The Arms.

Let the arms swing backward f
position, with the palm of the ha
the front; head raised. Say: "

Arms at the side in their natural position, palms toward the front; head straight. Say: "It is not so."

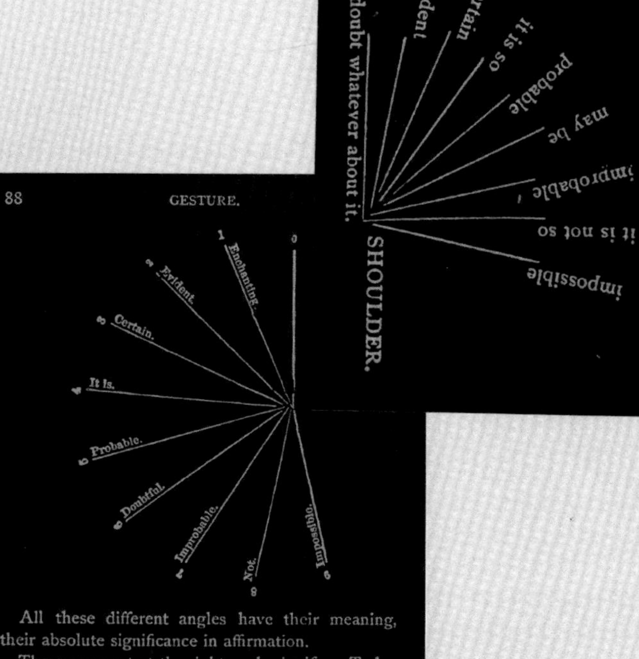

All these different angles have their meaning, their absolute significance in affirmation.

The movement at the right angle signifies: To be.

Lower: Perhaps.

Lower still: I doubt if it is so.

Lower: It is improbable.

Lower: It is not.

Lower: It is not possible.

Ascending: This is proven, I have the proof in my hand.

Higher: This is superlatively beautiful.

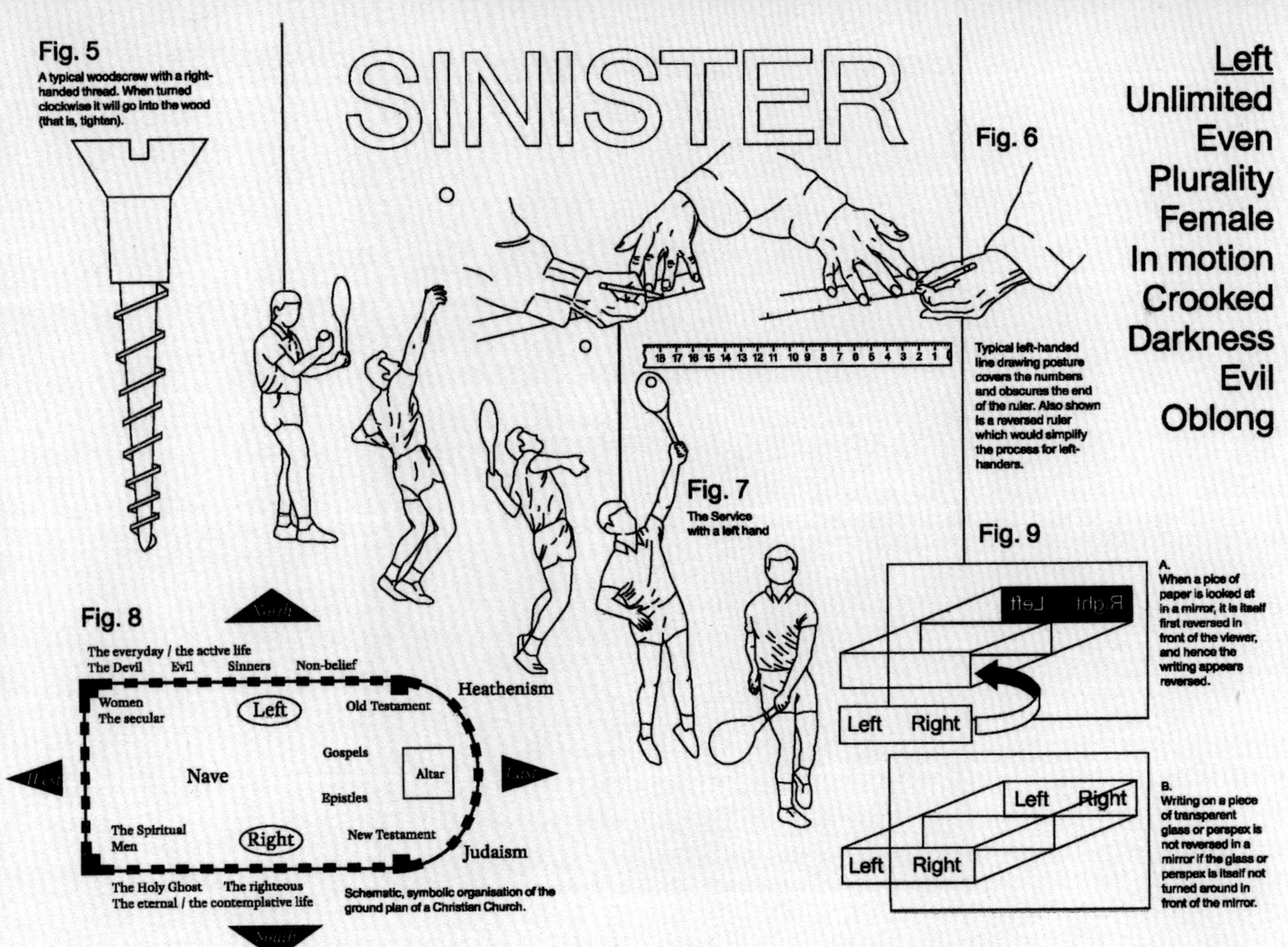

Part 3: Statues - Oratory Gestures - Right-handedness

Focusing on dictators' statues, oratory and gestures, I noted the frequently recurring raised-right-hand pose. This trait is common among statues of dictators and other political or historical figures, but why the right hand? In 2023, I had the opportunity to present an exhibition on the topic at the Mullae Art Factory in Seoul. *Dexter & Sinister* delves into the historical negative bias towards left-handedness, examining the symbolism of the left and right hand through graphics. *Dexter*, meaning "right" in Latin, and *sinister*, meaning "left", have historically conveyed the superiority of the right hand and the inferiority of the left hand. The project is a compilation of visual records that emphasise this dichotomy, using illustrations found in books from the mid to late 1900s.

The graphics on the *sinister* are created from guidebooks for left-handers such as Mark Brown's *Left Handed, Right Handed* (1979). The illustrations include items like left-handed scissors, methods for left-handers to play tennis, and explanations of how left-handers and right-handers develop different cognitive abilities due to the use of different brain hemispheres. By presenting these images from guidebooks intended for left-handers, the graphics aim to expose the social prejudices that hold up right-handedness as the norm.

Graphics: Ted Hyunhak Yoon, *Dexter & Sinister*, Commissioned by Jungeun Lee (curator) for the *Tabula Rasa* exhibition, South Korea, 2023

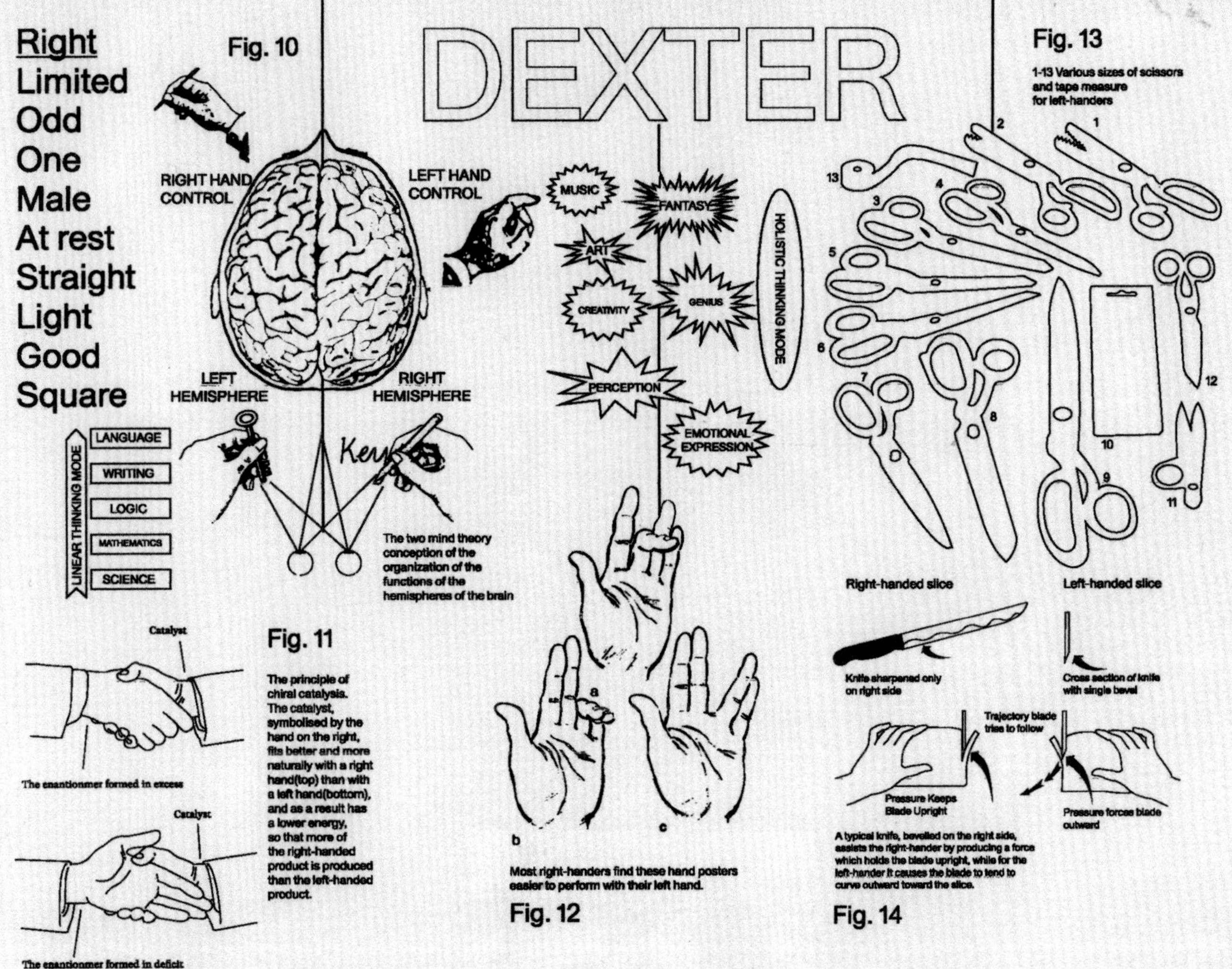

The graphics on the *dexter* consist of reinterpretations from the work of sociologist Robert Hertz, *Death and the Right Hand*, which provided insights into societal and religious perceptions of the right and left hands. Hertz defends the right hand's superiority by considering the anatomical reasons within the human body, the characteristics of social systems and environmental conditions outside the organism: *"What resemblance more perfect than that between our two hands! And yet, what a striking inequality there is! To the right hand go honours, flattering designations, prerogatives: it acts, orders, and takes. The left hand, on the contrary, is despised and reduced to the role of a humble auxiliary: by itself, it can do nothing; it helps, it supports, it holds. The right hand is the symbol and model of all aristocracy, the left hand of all common people. What are the titles of nobility of the right hand? And whence comes the servitude of the left?"*[1]

Layering modern images from the 1900s with the heraldic division of *dexter* and *sinister* from Western history, I aim to investigate the dualistic thinking behind our perception of the two hands and, by extension, both sides of the body. This project seeks to recontextualise the positive attributes associated with the right side and the negative attributes associated with the left, using a reconfigured parameter to navigate these metaphors and explore the binary ideologies that have shaped our understanding of human physiology and symbolism.

[1]p.335, Hertz, Robert. 1973. *"The pre-eminence of the right hand"* in *Right and Left: Essays on Dual Symbolic Classification*, translated by Rodney and Claudia Needham, edited by Rodney Needham, Reprint, *HAU: Journal of Ethnographic Theory 3 (2)*.

Images courtesy of

Mustapha

THE REALITY OF FISHMEAL AND OIL PRODUCTION IN THE GAMBIA

Manneh

Mustapha Manneh & Xaume Olleros

Once a striving fishing economy, The Gambia has seen a rapid and unchecked expansion in fishmeal factory operations in the last seven years. However, not all of its citizens are content with this expansion. Experts believe that fishmeal production was first introduced to the region to minimise fish wastage by using trimmed and rotten fish parts to produce fishmeal and oil. However, this is no longer the case as the fishmeal factories are now using fresh, small pelagic fish such as Sardinella and Bonga, which are consumed and in high demand by the local population, to produce their feeds and oil.

According to the Greenpeace Africa Report, in 2019, The Gambia had three fishmeal plants, Senegal had seven, and Mauritania had 40, although that number is since believed to have increased in Mauritania. Many reports have highlighted the fact that regional stocks of Bonga and Sardinella are now overexploited as a result of the existence of these Fishmeal plants, which, due to the high oil content found in these species, process tonnes of them every day to supply the global market. Unfortunately, however, these species were also traditionally the cheapest and most accessible fish for the local communities, who, due to the high demand from the fishmeal plants, now regard them as a luxury and have been forced to turn to frozen imported chicken.

The tiny West African nation of Gambia shares a frontier with Senegal and is one of the countries most impacted by the fishmeal boom. Its bountiful fish stocks have attracted hundreds of industrial trawlers from Asia, Europe, and Africa, and this expansion has come at the cost of the overexploitation of fish stocks and environmental pollution. The high numbers of foreign industrial fishing trawlers operating in Gambian waters has threatened the activities of local fishermen, fish dealers, and fish consumers, who are now fighting for survival. Moreover, the fishmeal plants contract local semi-industrial wooden Senegalese trawlers called Fela to fish for them, and the size of their nets leaves almost nothing in the sea.

The Gambia, commonly called the Smiling Coast of Africa, has 80 km of coastline, a population of 1.8 million, and is currently suffering from high levels of youth unemployment and political and social instability. It gained its independence from Britain in 1965 and has since relied on agriculture and tourism as its main source of income. The new government led by President Barrow, who was once described as an accidental president, succeeded the long-time dictator President Jammeh, who ruled from a West African regional body forced him out of power after he rejected the historic election of December 2016.

Chinese industrial trawlers dominate the country's government-controlled fishing waters, and these vessels often fish without proper monitoring by the authorities, who, at the same time, have been accused of taking bribes from fishing vessels caught fishing illegally. Furthermore, local fishermen have accused the authorities of adopting policies that only benefit the industrial trawlers. This lack of clear policies and regulations has put the artisanal fishing industry at risk, and there have been numerous conflicts between local and industrial trawlers. "Our nets are being destroyed by the big Chinese trawlers; we can't fight them because they have government support", says Lamin (whose name has been changed to protect his identity). The issue of net cutting by industrial trawlers is not uncommon in The Gambia and, in many cases, the victims can't access justice or compensation, forcing them out of the fishing sector. By law, industrial trawlers are not allowed to fish within nine nautical miles of the shore, but artisanal fishermen say the industrial trawlers are fishing up to four nautical miles from the coastline. Multiple local trawlers have complained about having their nets destroyed by the big Chinese industrial trawlers, in most cases receiving no compensation. More often than not, this is a result of conflict between the local artisanal vessels and the industrial trawlers.

In The Gambia, fishing is more than just a means to earn a living; for the Wolof and Serer peoples, it is an identity. For them, fighting for sustainable fishing means fighting to maintain their identity.

The Chinese government has played a hugely important role in the expansion of fishmeal processing in West Africa, with South-South Cooperation (SSC) heavily influencing the Chinese. Since the re-establishment of bilateral relations between The Gambia and China, three fishmeal factories have opened, and China has been actively involved in developing the local fishmeal sector and infrastructure. Chinese investors fully or partially control the country's three coastal fishmeal factories: Chinese-owned Golden Lead in Gunjur, which started operations in early 2016, followed by the joint Chinese-Mauritanian JXYG in Kartong in early 2017 and Nessim in Sanyang in 2018. China has a substantial market for fishmeal products due to its large-scale aquaculture industry.

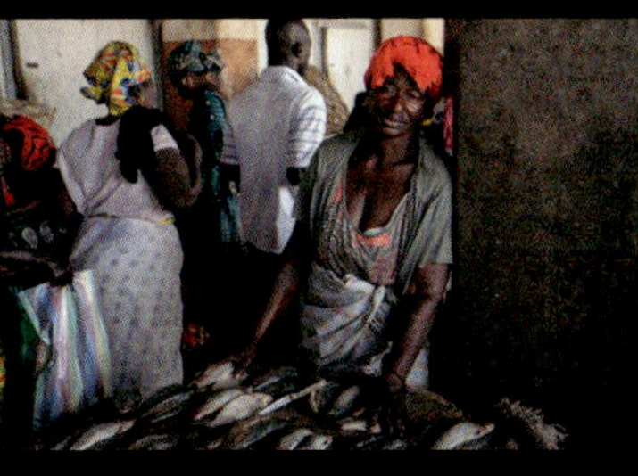

FISHMEAL PLANTS IN THE GAMBIA

In 2016, the settlement of Gunjur welcomed the first fishmeal plant called Golden Lead Factory, but the idea was not well understood at that initial stage.

The arrival of the fishmeal industry has brought social, economic, and environmental issues to the region. There is rising unemployment among the area’s young people, who are losing their livelihoods to fishmeal and overfishing and consequently increasingly view migration to Europe as the only way to succeed. "The Europeans are taking all our fish; we will go to their countries and take all their jobs too", says Alieu.

The community rebelled against the fishmeal plant after experiencing the toxic odour generated when it discharged wastewater into the lagoon, killing the resident aquatic species. According to Lamin Jassey, sustainable fishing is both important and necessary in The Gambia because "it will increase opportunities for the community and ensure the protection of endangered species". The Gambia, encircled by Senegal with its borders curving around the beautiful River Gambia, is Africa's smallest nation. Yet, despite its size, it has become well known for the mass fishmeal operations rapidly expanding along its coastline. "I am extremely concerned about the future of The Gambia, and arresting me won't change my position. I see it as normal. The fishing industry contributes a lot to The Gambia's GDP, but the introduction of fishmeal has affected the market value and people are finding it hard to access fish and losing their jobs", adds Jassey.

Two respective investigations by international NGOs – Greenpeace International and the Changing Markets Foundation – have cautioned that the scale of Gambia's fishmeal and oil production is unsustainable and the country's food stocks will be in danger if the initiative is not properly managed. Greenpeace Africa's "A Waste of Fish" report, published in June 2019, analyses the consequences of fishmeal processing in The Gambia, Senegal and Mauritania, a region in which 50 fishmeal plants have been opened in recent years. It calculated that 4.5 fresh fish are needed to make just 1 kg of fishmeal powder. The research also established that neither the FAO nor the Gambian government have a record of the fishmeal production and exportation that has been taking place in The Gambia for the last seven years. The Fishing For Catastrophe investigation highlighted the strong links between fishmeal and oil production in The Gambia and China, the world's largest aqua-feed producer, while at the same time predicting that demand for feed for farmed fish will see exponential growth in the coming decades.

THE IMPACT OF FISHMEAL ON TOURISM

Since fishmeal factories are located in coastal regions for easy access to fishery resources, they have also prevented tourism workers from accessing the beach. As Said Jatta, a juice bar operator, explains, “As a juice presser, the people who buy our juices are mostly tourists, but today, the fishmeal operations nearby have had a devastating impact. We are here because we have a business, but the fishmeal indus-

try is polluting the entire place. I do not support the fishmeal sector… who knows what the after-effects of inhaling all those awful smells will be…" Jatta believes that the government should focus on developing tourism rather than supporting the growth of the fishmeal industry. Unfortunately, despite tourism in the area being promoted as a sustainable and eco-friendly business, the proximity of the fishmeal operations has made many tourist businesses unviable: the smells, the waste being discharged into the ocean where tourists swim, and beaches littered with rotten fish have all impacted the sector. The Gambian tourism industry is collapsing, with hundreds leaving the sector and many young people being put out of business. Fishing and tourism are the two primary sources of youth employment in coastal Gambia and provide the most prominent source of income for poor rural households. As a result, advocates maintain that no serious government would construct or permit fishmeal operations close to developed tourist areas, as the two businesses are so clearly incompatible.

Even though the Gambian government has attempted to industrialise the fisheries industry by promoting fishmeal and industrial fishing to increase employment opportunities in the sector, these policies appear to benefit very few while causing significant damage to the other major sector, tourism. Many of the jobs created are non-skilled positions, such as manual labour or security and porter roles, and in return, the traditional fishing and tourism sectors are being destroyed. Moreover, even talking about fishmeal and unsustainable fishing can land activists in jail, with dozens of youths arrested for planning a demonstration against the Golden Lead fishmeal factory in Gunjur, many of whom described their arrest as politically motivated.

THE UNFULFILLED PROMISES

In their effort to promote fisheries, the Gambian government, through its development agency GIEPA, is giving tax breaks to fishmeal and oil companies in return for the creation of jobs. Understanding African dynamics and the need for employment opportunities, investors who never invest have utilised these opportunities to exploit Africa, and the communities with fishmeal resources were given empty promises. According to Ahmed Manjang, "The people of Gunjur allowed the fishmeal factory to be established in its current location on the condition that the factory would provide six hundred jobs as promised by the factory owners and that they would build a fish market for the local women who previously used the allocated land to process and dry fish. They also promised to build a road to link the fishing village with the main town of Gunjur. As of today, none of these agreements have been honoured, and worse still, the factory owners have leased the property

village authorities".

A medically-trained microbiologist believes that fighting the fishmeal factories in The Gambia is hugely challenging because of the endemic corruption in the country, accusing the senior government officials who are supposed to regulate the excesses of these factories of being corrupt and arguing that it is now up to local activists to challenge these powerful multinational factories. "Just recently a local activist made a social media post to engage local fisheries officers, the local fisheries management committee and the fishmeal operator on the subject of the increasing quantity of juvenile fish being caught in Gunjur. The local fisheries department immediately informed the fisheries minister, who alerted the police commissioner. The matter was then referred to the local police department who wasted no time in inviting the local activist in for questioning. Two days later, Interpol questioned him in relation to the same social media post, and they did not stop there; the paramilitary was deployed to Gunjur beach for a fortnight in anticipation of civil action by local activists". He further stated that these are just some of the intimidation tactics being used by the government to frustrate and intimidate.

Over the past decade, there has been a continuous decline in the number of fish being landed at all major fish landing sites in The Gambia and unless something is done quickly our fish stocks are at risk of complete collapse. The Gambia is still behind when it comes to data on its pelagic fish stock, and as the catch sizes reduce, the size of the nets used by trawlers increase. "We need strong institutions to enforce proper fishing regulations. As of now, I'm not hopeful of finding a solution to this menace", says Lamin Jassey.

THE COMMUNITY COURT CASE AGAINST FISHMEAL

In 2017, the Golden Lead fishmeal plant in Gunjur deliberately discharged wastewater into the Bolong Fenyo Lagoon, resulting in the deaths of all its aquatic species and prompting the Gambian Environmental Agency to sue the Chinese-owned Golden Lead fishmeal factory for its actions. The case did not proceed well until the Gambian government intervened, which led to an out-of-court settlement and allowed the factory's operations to continue. The Gambian government claimed that taking the fishmeal company to court would have dissuaded other investors from investing in the country. These out-of-court settlements were negotiated without community involvement, and the Golden Lead company was also accused of withholding information about its waste management and not keeping proper records. The company was asked to pay a bond of 25,000 US dollars, take immediate measures to deal with its wastewater, and pay for the testing of waters that had already been polluted.

In 2018, several young people from Gunjur decided to remove a waste pipe from the Atlantic Ocean. The police arrested and charged the six leaders of the team: Alhagie Bojang, Omar Darboe, Ousman Sanneh, Lamin Jassey, Foday Karl Darboe, and Amadou Scattered Janneh, the former Gambian information minister. The criminal case brought by the Inspector General of Police alleged that the six environmentalists had removed waste disposal pipes used by the Golden Lead fishmeal processing plant to dispose its waste into the sea. In 2018, the Gunjur environmental activists and their lawyer sued the Golden Lead factory for discharging its untreated waste into the ocean via a pipe hidden by mangroves, but their case has yet to be called before a high court judge in Banjul. Many believe the case is being deliberately delayed due to political reasons. The activists maintain that litigation is the only way to stop the environmental damage being caused by the fishmeal industry.

A REGIONAL PERSPECTIVE ON THE FISHMEAL INDUSTRY

A similar movement has been gaining momentum in the neighbouring country of Senegal. Environmentalists are calling for a more regional approach to campaigns against the fishmeal plants, with experts pointing out that individual countries will not be able to negotiate a better fisheries deal with the EU or China alone and arguing, therefore, that regional collaboration is essential. With a population of just 1.8 million, the chances of The Gambia successfully negotiating an improved fisheries deal with either China or the EU are minimal.

Additionally, the fishmeal factories in both countries have had little regard for environmental

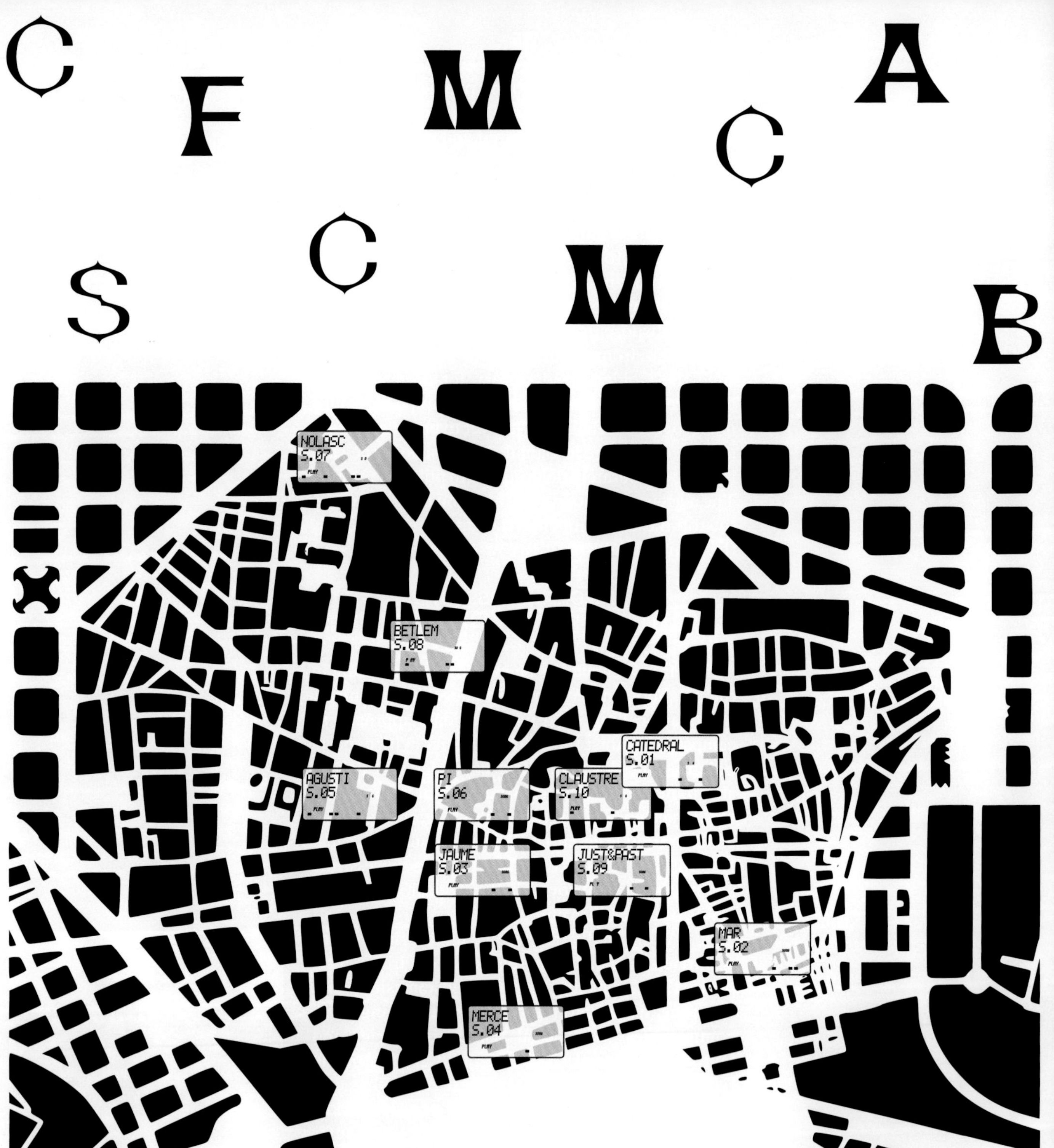

CSFCMMCAB is the initials of *Correspondències Simbòliques entre Folklore Catòlic i Música Màkina al Casc Antic de Barcelona* (Symbolic Correspondences between Catholic Folklore and *Màkina* Music in the Old Quarter of Barcelona). This is a research project that uses music production as a way of working. It springs from the anthropological parallels between the two epochal polarities of a particular local folkloric continuum: popular religious belief (post-hegemonic, Catholic culture) and electronic music (proto-hegemonic, *màkina* [hardcore techno] culture). This is just the starting point. The project moves beyond these anthropological parallels to focus strictly on the other parallels revealed through the exact science of musical symbolism or speculative music (an expression coined by Joscelyn Godwin). The initial methodology thus consisted of bringing together various such systems. They were then tested to find out the possibilities they offered to translate Barcelona's (previously inventoried) Catholic iconography into electronic music and/or vice versa.

The most useful system was Claudius Ptolemy's tonal zodiac. This ultimately establishes a correspondence between the annual cycle and the Greek *disdiapason* (two octaves of our diatonic scale). Taking this idea to its logical limit, I divided the two octaves into 360 micro-notes with an interval of 0.07 tones (a 180 TET microtonal scale). A micro-note was thus obtained for each zodiacal degree and day of the year. This made it possible to assign a micro-note to each saint or dedication in the Catholic calendar of saints' days based on the date of their feast day. I also discovered the tradition of *goigs*, local folk songs dedicated to each saint. This tradition works in itself as a system of musical symbolism because the *goigs* are sung on the specific saint's day in the specific place where they are venerated. By applying these two systems to the set of saints displayed inside churches, I obtained a compositional formula that allows the churches to be transformed into songs. The architectural structure would determine the musical structure: each chapel would become a rhythm, the bass line would play the micro-note corresponding to each saint's day, and the melody of their *goigs* would play over the top (transposed to a key containing one of the degrees of that micro-note). The rest of the musical elements would be selected from the inventory of formulaic characteristics typical of the *màkina* style. This criterion followed was subjective synaesthesia between the sensation of space and nuances of frequency. I selected the case studies with this formula in mind: ten churches in the Old Quarter of Barcelona that had a clearly serial arrangement of saints' chapels. Using this compositional method, I turned them into the ten tracks in *Vol. 1: Santoral Interior*. The disc was published in CD format with a *BCN Producció* grant from La Capella art centre.

I used a single device to produce the music: the Korg Electribe EMX-1. This is the device with which, starting in 2009, I began making electronic music without a computer for the *Coàgul* project. It is a music station that combines nine drumbox tracks with five synthesiser tracks, which can be simultaneously sequenced in multitrack patterns that can then be chained together to form songs. On the one hand, I liked the idea of all the sound coming from a single source. This results in a natural compactness that tends to be more difficult to achieve when produced with different digital or analogue instrumental sources. On the other hand, the structural logic implicit in this device was a perfect way for me to construct the music in correspondence with churches' architecture. Thus, each pattern would correspond to one chapel. Synthesiser track 1 would be the bass and the other four would be melodies, one for each of the *goigs* of each saint displayed in that chapel (the higher ones had a higher and more ethereal sound, and those closer to the ground had a deeper, more solid sound). I could thus chain together, in song mode, all of the desired patterns in the order in which the chapels are laid out in real space, giving rise to each church-song. The signs shown on the map reproduce the device's screen as it appears when it shows each of the songs. As for tuning, the Korg EMX-1 has a temperament adjustment parameter; each synth track can be tuned to within hundredths of a tone. This allowed me to tune the five tracks in each pattern to the micro-tonality of the corresponding micro-note for the saint's day.

For five years before starting the project, I worked in the Barcelona Cathedral cloister shop. There I immersed myself in the culture of the saints. I tried to approach it based on the Kabbalistic knowledge I had long been familiar with. The idea of heterotopic spaces and memory palaces, which I was steeped in while writing my master's thesis, also determined my view of all the serial ensembles that made up the various layers of cathedral architecture. I could say that carrying out this project went hand-in-hand with my spiritual maturation: the more I delved into tradition, the more I longed to take part in it. This led me to rediscover faith and Catholic practice. During this process I moved away from esotericism as I came to understand the theological divergence between the Gnostic path and Catholic doctrine. Thus, the zodiacal basis of the compositional method used for *Santoral Interior* has remained as a reduced fractal image of paganism that inevitably served as a bridge to the revelation of Christ. It also reflects, on a small scale, this historical tension that lasts to this day. In a sense, this project exemplifies, for me, the ideological nuance in which I want to circumscribe my production as an artist: I want to propose an archetypal art in a pre-modern sense. The aim is not to criticise but instead to celebrate eternal values, constructing it with forms and methods specific to the contemporary world. It is not a rereading of tradition to adapt it to the present; it is a rereading of the present to realign it with tradition. And as Gustav Mahler said, "Tradition is not the worship of ashes, but the transmission of fire."

Each church map acts as the score for the corresponding song. Inside each chapel one can see compartments in which the micro-notes corresponding to the feast days of the saints they house are written. For example: "F#'+27" means that at that point there is an image of Santa Rita, because this is the micro-note for 22 May, that saint's feast day. The black boxes refer to solar calendar feast days. The white boxes refer to lunar calendar feast days (Good Friday, Corpus Christi, Sacred Heart, etc.). They contain micro-notes that correspond to their solar dates in the year 2020. When the maps are understood in this way, the order in which the songs are played is analogous to the route that a hypothetical visitor would take when visiting the chapels in a Western reading order (left to right). They start by going through the door (bottom centre), which sounds like an intro with little percussion. They continue, ascending on the left (the Gospel side), where all the rhythms corresponding to the set of chapels on this side play. They reach the high altar area (upper central area), which sounds like an interlude with the melody of the saint or dedication as the build-up. They move on, descending on the right (the Epistle side), where all the rhythms of the chapels on this side play. They finally going back out of the door with the corresponding final micro-note. For churches that have a nave (S.01 and S.02), the saint or dedication is in the diametrical centre. In the song's timeline, the titular saint's melody is superimposed on the others. This is repeated during all the rhythms of all the chapels along the nave, since the saint honorarily presides over them. Due to its size, I composed two different songs for the cathedral: one for the basilica (S.01) and the other for the cloister (S.10). The order of play for the cloister begins at the door leading to the street (Santa Eulàlia, in the centre of the upper side). It continues in the same direction, from left to right, circling until it ends at the same point. If one wished to go through the entirety of the building, one could change the track to one of the two rhythms for the doors that connect the basilica to the cloister (in the fold separating the two pages) and link up –in a hypothetical mix– with the rhythm for the other part of the building.

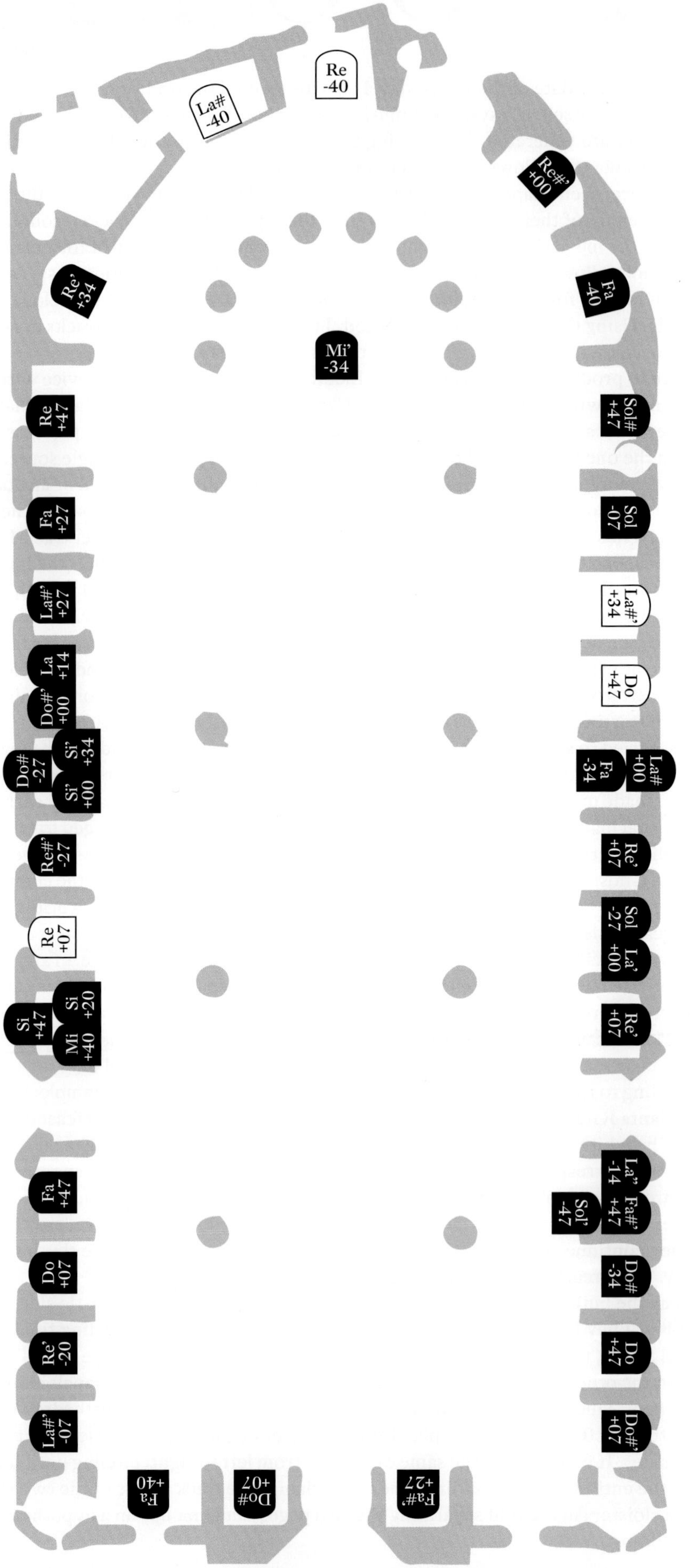

Re -40
La# -40
Re#' +00
Re' +34
Fa -40
Mi' -34
Re +47
Sol# +47
Fa +27
Sol -07
La#' +27
La#' +34
La +14
Do +47
Do# +00
Si' +34
Do# -27
Si' +00
Fa -34
La# +00
Re#' -27
Re' +07
Sol -27
La' +00
Re +07
Si +47
Si +20
Mi +40
Re' +07
La' -14
Fa#' +47
Sol' -47
Fa +47
Do +07
Do# -34
Re' -20
Do +47
La#' -07
Do#' +07
Fa +40
Do# +07
Fa#' +27

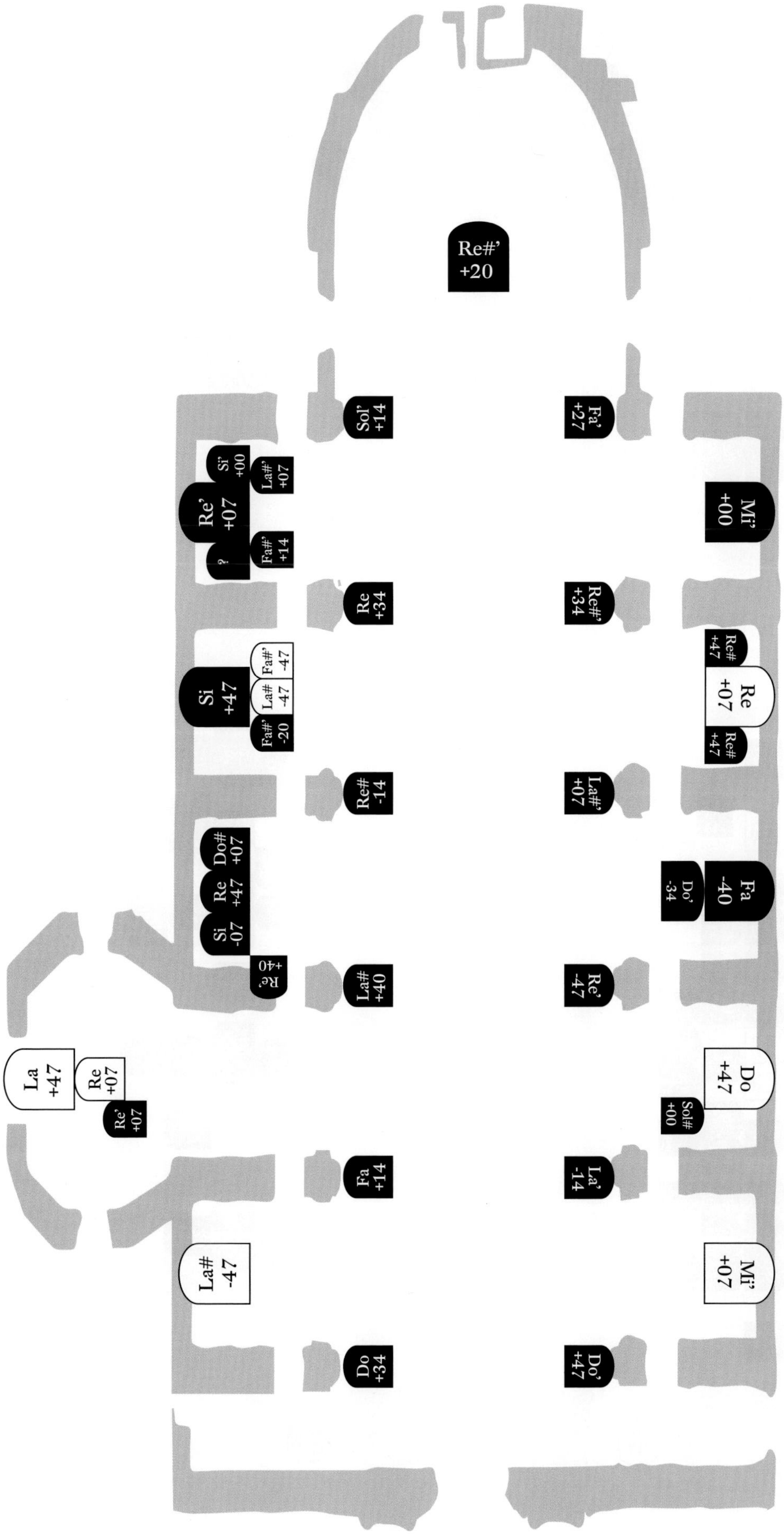

Re#'
+20
Sol' +14
Fa' +27
Si' +00
La#' +07
Re' +07
Fa#' +14
?
Mi' +00
Re +34
Re#' +34
Fa#' -47
La# -47
Si +47
Fa#' -20
Re# +47
Re +07
Re# +47
Re# -14
La#' +07
Do# +07
Re +47
Si -07
Re' +40
Fa -40
Do' -34
La# +40
Re' -47
La +47
Re +07
Re' +07
Do +47
Sol# +00
Fa +14
La' -14
La# -47
Mi' +07
Do +34
Do' +47

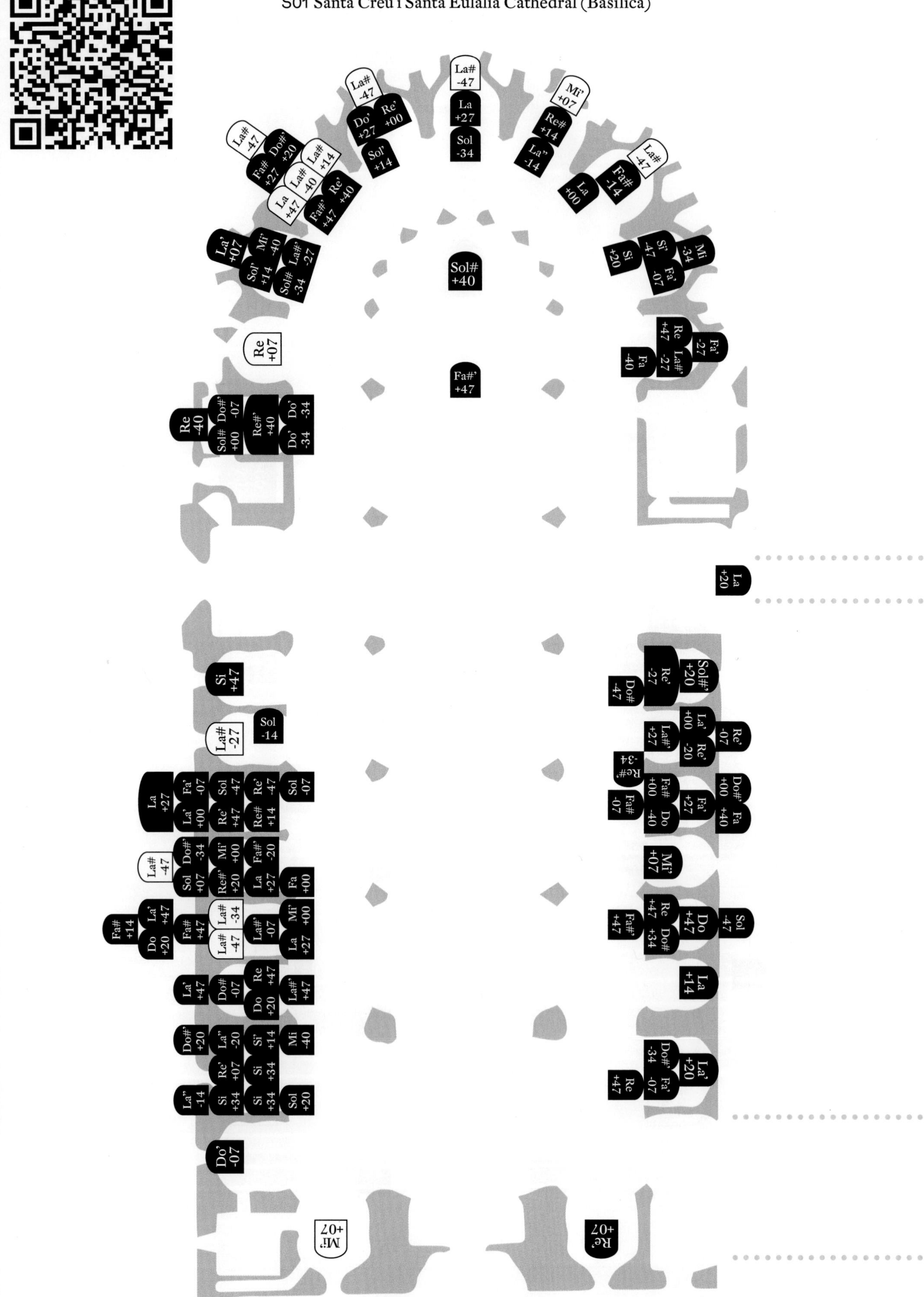

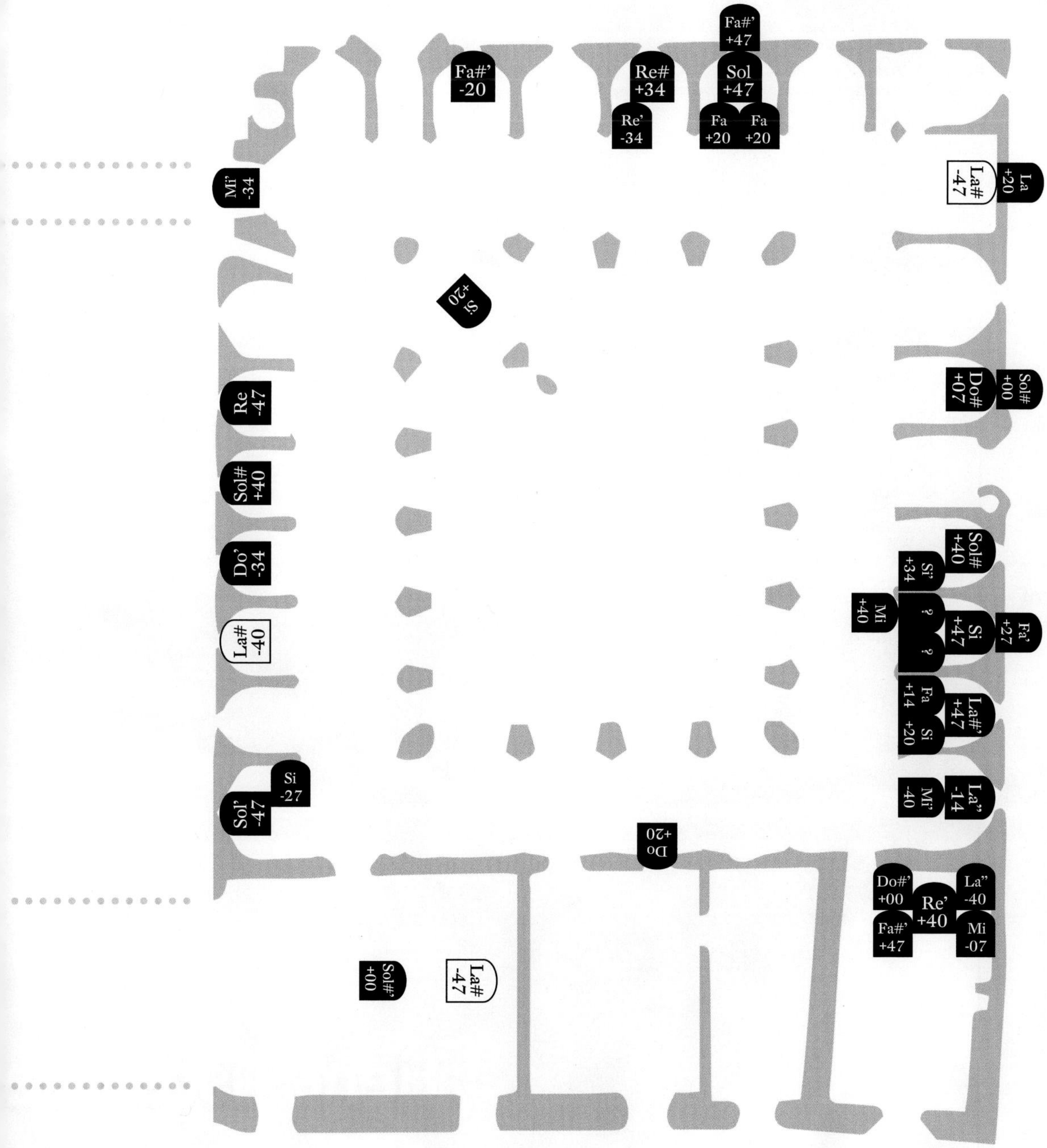
Fa#' +47
Fa#' -20
Re# +34
Sol +47
Re' -34
Fa +20
Fa +20
La +20
La# -47
Mi' -34
Si +20
Sol# +00
Do# +07
Re -47
Sol# +40
Do' -34
La# -40
Sol# +40
Si' +34
Mi +40
?
Si +47
Fa' +27
?
Fa +14
La#' +47
Si +20
Mi' -40
La'' -14
Si -27
Sol' -47
Do +20
Do#' +00
Re' +40
La'' -40
Fa#' +47
Mi -07
Sol# +00
La# -47

[comes from page 07]

M.U. It's not that I can't understand sex without love, it's just that I'm too aware of my own discontinuity so as not to prefer sex with love to sex without love. That doesn't mean that I don't enjoy eroticism of the body. But eroticism of the body seems to me to be something sinister, something cynical and selfish. However, eroticism of the heart seems freer to me. It gives me a great fear of death. It terrifies me and makes me panic. I think about it constantly. And only when I make love, only in eroticism of the heart am I able or capable of forgetting and freeing myself of it. That moment is also when I become fully aware, when I am fully aware of that freedom. And I even tell myself, "I'm not afraid of death right now." And I don't mean I feel immortal or something like that, nonsense like that, no. But a sort of clean and calm feeling that's continuous. That's what happens to me when... or at least I think that's what happens to me when I'm in love, when I fall in love. Feeling and believing it. Accepting one's own death. However, the fear of dying is then replaced by a passion that has a meaning even more violent than death itself.

J. Could you comprehend passion without love?

Miguel, Nuria. 2009. 2 Leona come cebra. Retrieved September 9, 2024 from https://www.youtube.com/watch?v=GQFcL9hisxs

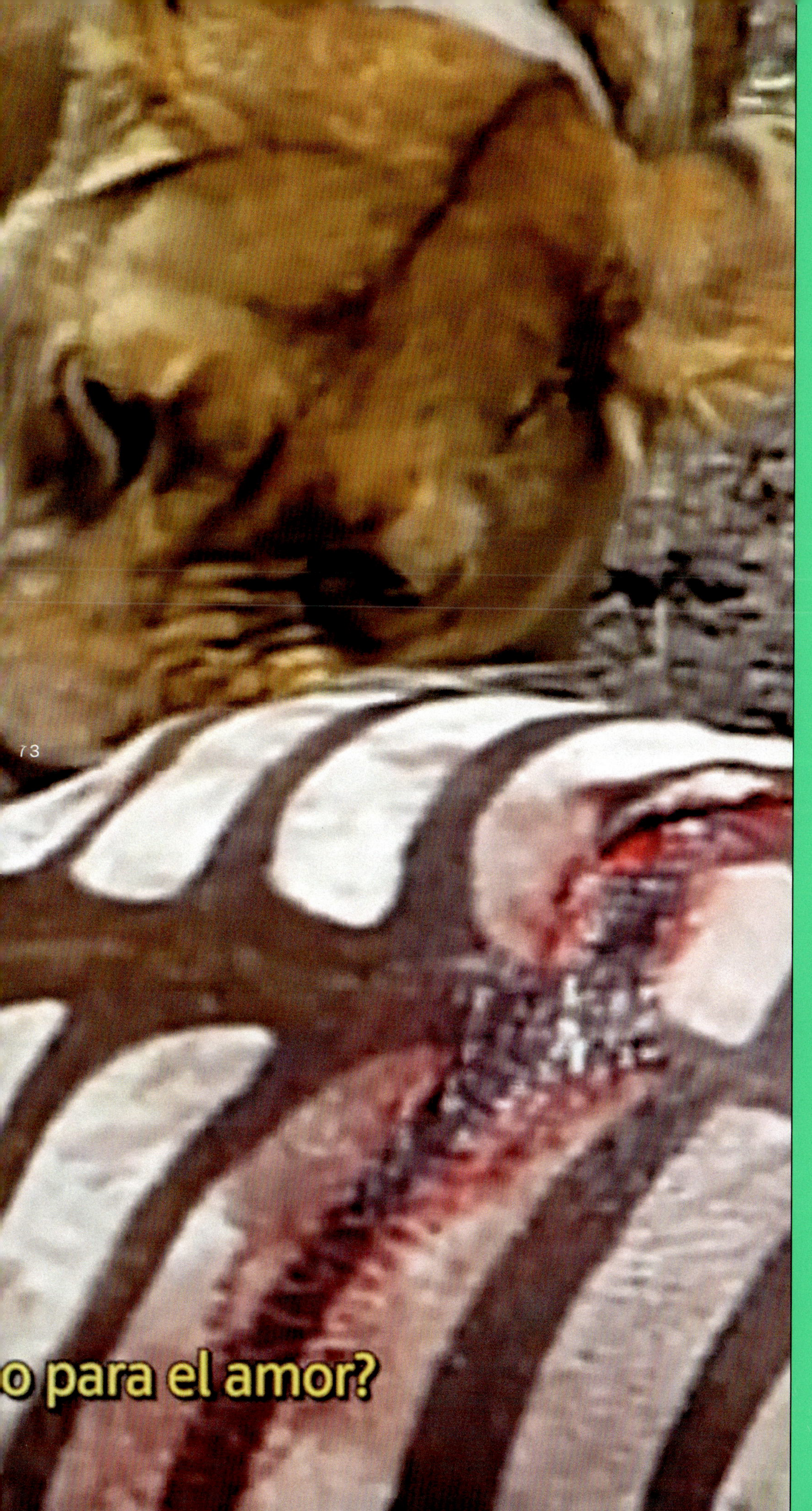

M.U. No, I couldn't.

J. What about sex without passion?

M.U. Yes, of course. Unfortunately, sex can be horribly dispassionate.

J. What do you think about prostitution? Do you condemn it or support it?

M.U. I believe that neither condemnation nor support are concepts that do justice to prostitution.

J. What have you gained by being chosen Miss Universe?

M.U. A crown, a cloak, a sash... fame... money... sexual capital... Ornaments that highlight the erotic value of the object.

J. Are you happy?

M.U. Yes. Being a woman is a luxury.

J. And being a man?

M.U. A judgement that both men and women suffer from. It's not like we're any more desirable than men, but women put care and effort into preserving our beauty. For us, for other women, and to suggest ourselves as objects for the aggressive desire of men. At least that makes us more powerful. And braver.

J. Are you a feminist?

M.U. Yes, why? For me, feminism is voluptuousness in its maximum power and exuberance.

J. What is beauty in your opinion?

M.U. In an object, beauty is what expresses desire.

J. Do you suffer from it?

M.U. Yes.

J. Would you like to kill beauty, like desire?

M.U. As I told you before, prohibition lives in humiliation and outrage through transgression.

J. A few days ago, some photographs were published in which you were seen crying and drying your tears with €50, €100, and €200 bills. Some media outlets considered the controversy to be a real scandal. You were highly criticized. Did it affect you?

M.U. I guess they should have been €500 bills, right? Clearly. Everything and nothing affects me about a society that is extremely moralistic and humourless, it's inevitable.

J. Why were you crying?

M.U. Because… I got emotional listening to a song that reminded me of my childhood, my family and my friends.

J. A political song?

M.U. All songs are political as well as poetic. I am more excited by the poetic sensibility than the political one, the one

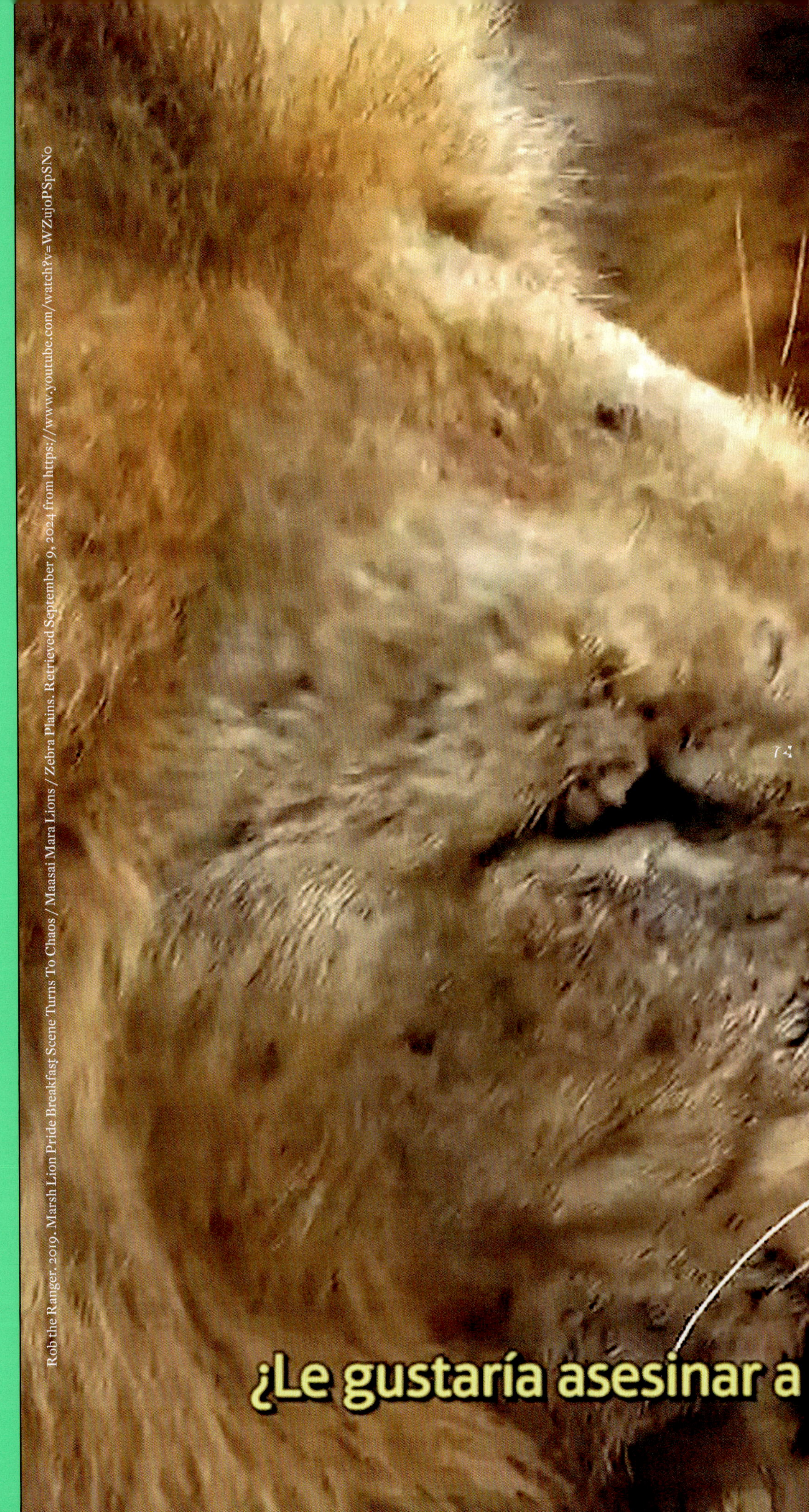

Rob the Ranger, 2019. Marsh Lion Pride Breakfast Scene Turns To Chaos / Maasai Mara Lions / Zebra Plains. Retrieved September 9, 2024 from https://www.youtube.com/watch?v=WZujoPSpSNo

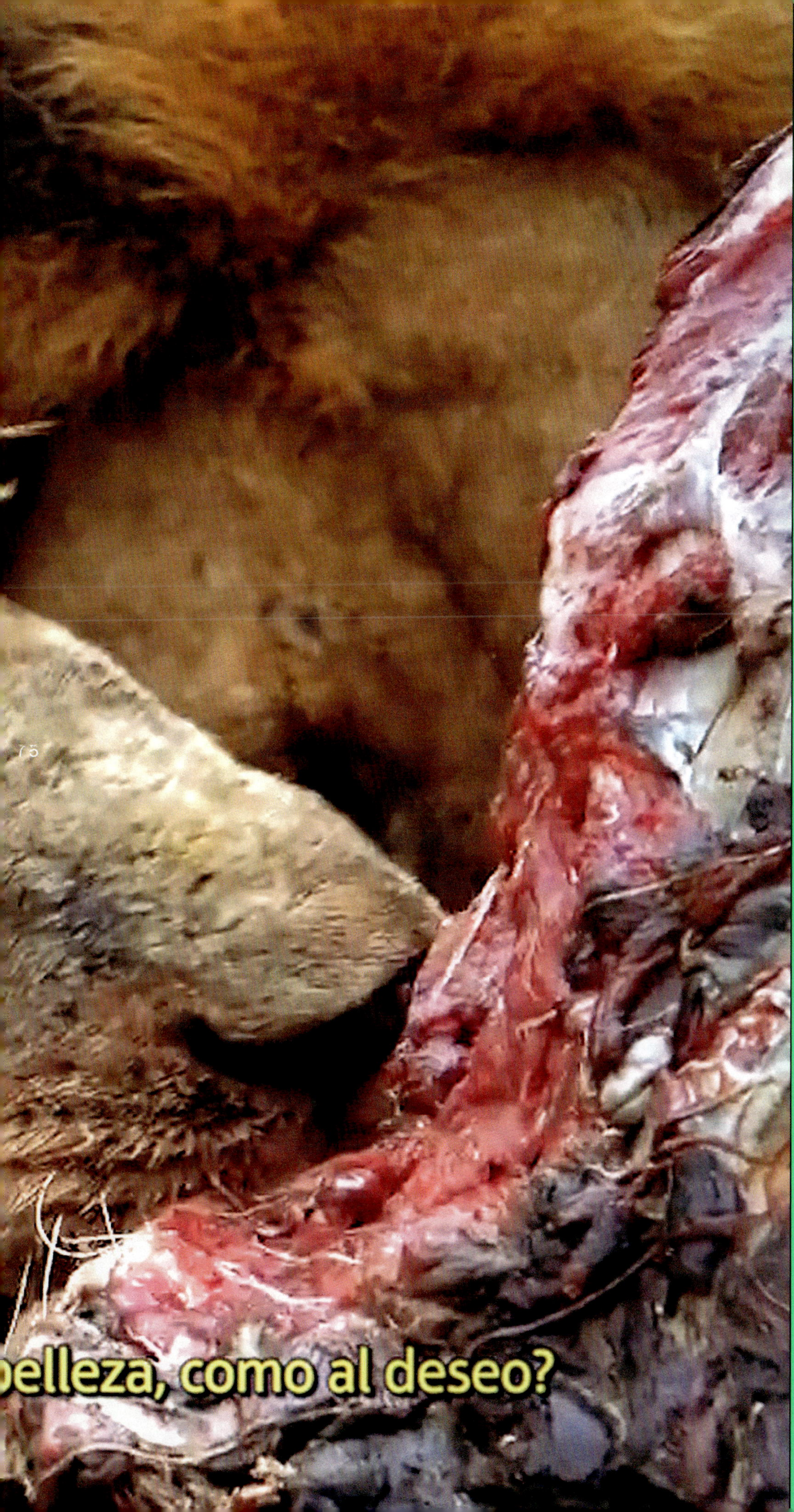

that truly violates the human spirit.

J. What is the human spirit in your opinion?

M.U. The human spirit is a panopticon from which one can contemplate the sacred and the profane, the pure and impure, order and disorder, even obscenity. God is no less obscene than human beings. Both have failed because… I don't know, they've probably failed one another due to their pride. I know that the human spirit is just as much of an imprisonment as the human body. But the spirit contains everything: good and evil. And everyone is free to desecrate themselves or be consecrated. Or even to make a consecration through desecration.

J. Do you believe in God?

M.U. Yes, definitely. I'm an erotic object.

To others, the universe seems decent because decent people have gelded eyes. That is why they fear lewdness. They are never frightened by the crowing of a rooster or when strolling under a starry heaven. In general, people savor the 'pleasures of the flesh' only on condition that they be insipid.

GEORGES BATAILLE

belleza, como al deseo?

@omarh

Two friends are amidst the war

erzshow

in an adventure
towards successS

In recent years, a new trend has flourished among some popular media platforms. Condé Nast's *Vogue* launched a video series titled "In The Bag," where celebrities, singers, actors and actresses, designers and socialites show the essential objects they carry in their purses. Another platform, GQ, released a YouTube series also featuring celebrities; in this case, guests are asked to share the "10 Things They Can't Live Without". Asking millionaires about their "essentials" and their "can't live without things" has always felt a bit awkward, as if within their privileged lives, sharing their essential objects will contribute to a better understanding of contemporary humankind and its survival necessities. Following that trend, we have approached Gazan bloggers Mohammed and Omar to contribute with a video-review of 10 essential objects they can't live without in the ongoing occupation and genocide in Gaza.